FORGIVEN

Matthew Whittington

Humudi & Micah.
Thank you for all your support.
I hope you find my lessons and
message helpful. — *Matt W*

CLC Publishing
Books with Purpose

Always find Peace in
the Pain
Matt W

Copyright © 2019 by Matthew Whittington

All rights reserved. No part of this book may be used or reproduced in any manner whatsoever without written permission of the author.

While this is a work of non-fiction, where necessary fictional names have been used.

Published by CLC Publishing, LLC.
Mustang, OK, 73064

Printed in the United States of America

Book Design by Shannon Whittington
Cover Design by Dillon Cooper

ISBN: 978-0-578-44393-5

Non-Fiction/Self-Help
Addiction/Recovery

02.04.19

For Ryker

"It's what you learn after you know it all that counts." - John Wooden

Forward

I'm Mac Mullings and I am a grateful alcoholic. Now, that's not the way I thought I would be introducing myself to you. If you asked the 9-year-old me, my name would be accompanied by "starting fullback for the Denver Broncos" or something. Recovery was not a community I had planned to be part of but I wouldn't trade it for anything. Without sobriety I have nothing.

You'll never hear me say that I have things figured out. In my opinion, we addicts live with that mentality and we are asking for trouble. However, I can share with you how my darkest moment of isolation became the brightest revelation. Since then, the motto of "Finding Peace in the Pain" has been engraved in my being.

Prior to December 22nd, 2016, guilt, shame, resentment and fear were the four chambers that pumped my broken heart. Life was full of pints instead of prayer. Liquor instead of love. Hangovers instead of hope. I had lost jobs, relationships and eventually the will to live. My addiction had led me to a point of spiritual bankruptcy and we were closing the account. When you hear someone is in that place you may ask "what were you thinking?!!" and the answer for me was that I wasn't. I was on autopilot. Checked out. Just like a horse wears blinders during a race to keep their focus on the path before them, that is where my thoughts were taking me. I didn't see the pictures of my beautiful family around the house. I saw a pond outside my back porch, and paired with the alcohol that I had been consuming for 4 days, my mind began to entertain ways to get the job done. Thinking of it now still makes me shake my head and give thanks for not being there anymore. We don't regret where we came from but we sure as hell refuse to go back.

Despair is a blessing in these moments.

I've always been someone that can overthink things. I try to figure it out. Analyze it.

Looking back maybe that's why I enjoyed the game 'Clue' so much. But when it comes to the night of my rock bottom, I don't even question what occurred. It was divine intervention that made me reach out and call for help. I've had people tell me I was nuts for calling 911 on myself but can you get any crazier than wanting to drown yourself in your backyard? I believe that when it comes to addiction, surrender is the greatest victory. Ever since I waved that white flag and let God take over my life it has been nothing short of miraculous. As John Newton so beautifully wrote in 'Amazing Grace', "he saved a wretch like me".

Just like I had earned my spot in the meeting rooms and clubhouses of various recovery programs, I had earned my seat in the therapist's office. One in particular stared at me as if trying to decide whether to throat punch me or not and simply asked, "Why are you playing with it? Why is your obvious addiction to alcohol a game to you?" I stopped my verbal diarrhea of excuses long enough to cross my arms and sit back. Then she said it: "Tell me about your daughter". I was silent. The boulder that formed in my throat made it impossible to speak.

I always wanted to be a dad but this particular time in my life I felt like I was falling very short of deserving the title. The intention was there but the execution was not. Sure, I would watch the Disney movies and wear a tiara during tea parties but a drink was always near. I'm singing 'Frozen' songs at the top of my lungs while walking to the kitchen to pour something else on the ice rattling in my rocks glass. As much as I didn't want it to be, that was an often occurrence and the guilt tore me up inside. Most of my adult life I had associated drinking with having fun and here I was trying to incorporate that idea into Daddy/Daughter time. The addict mentality will have us believe that there is absolutely nothing wrong with that scenario. "I'm not driving around with her in the car! We are at home and I am just having a couple of drinks!". Then what happens when we run out of booze? "The store actually isn't *that* far and just a little bit more will do". The obsession will hijack our mind.

One vivid memory I have is standing at the kitchen sink and talking to my daughter while she was in her walker. After a series of googly faces I put a bottle of warm gut rot vodka to my mouth and took a swig. As quickly as it went in, it came right back out. Unfortunately, that would be the first of many times I would become sick in front of her.

Alcohol was not my problem, but rather my solution, to a list of things I tried to run from. One of them being the feeling of failure as a parent. I had this very real fear that God would punish my daughter for my shortcomings. As if He would get tired of my second chances and teach me a lesson by harming her. Man, what a horrible misinterpretation of God's love. Having that drive my thoughts was crippling. I began to hate the person I saw in the mirror.

"Resentment destroys the container that carries it".

That statement could not be more true, especially when people like myself are feeding addiction. We are emotional hoarders. "Let go and let God" is just something we see on coffee mugs and coasters. You see, *forgiveness* is an 'F' word the addict does not favor. That would require us to embrace feelings instead of running the other way. We would have to stop playing the "victim card" and most unsettling, we would have to learn to forgive ourselves. It's a tough onion to peel, no doubt, but when the dead layers start to fall away it's pretty damn beautiful. We learn to take a breath and realize that we are not defined by the mistakes of our past.

I accept that while practicing in my alcoholism I was not the person that my creator intended for me to be. Life still happens but if I hit my knees every morning and cast all my cares on him, it will continue to be better than imagined.

*God grant me the serenity
to accept the things I cannot change;
courage to change the things I can;
and wisdom to know the difference.
Living one day at a time;
enjoying one moment at a time;
accepting hardships as the pathway to peace;
taking, as He did, this sinful world
as it is, not as I would have it;
trusting that He will make all things right
if I surrender to His will;
that I may be reasonably happy in this life
and supremely happy with Him forever in the next. Amen.*

I love Matt Whittington and was moved to tears when he asked me to contribute to this book. FORGIVEN is a powerful story of how addiction is a disease that affects the entire family. Emotionally imprisoning all of those involved. Matt's perspective of being the child of an alcoholic brings the process of understanding to a whole new level. Anger is replaced by acceptance. Loathing with love. Frustration with forgiveness.

I encourage you to soak in the words and reflect on how they may be applied in your life. Do that and you will experience what it is to find 'Peace in the Pain'.

Introduction

During the six months I worked on this book there were a lot of tears. Frequently I sat in reflection for long periods of time to ponder the words that needed to be said. Frankly, the transparency I've given to each person who reads this was very scary to me. Who's going to be mad at me? How are people going to digest my story and interpret the lessons I've learned along the way? In particular, I struggled the most early on in the process. I was scared about what my family would think more than anything. With a little urging, it became apparent that this is my story, and it is important.

To tell this story right, for the full powerful effect, I had to be transparent. In order to understand why forgiveness is so difficult, especially for me, there has to be honest disclosure. You have to understand the pain. While I had initially feared that telling this story is somehow cowardly in her death and diminishes her life and memory, I believe the opposite is not only possible, but far more probable. What I believe I have accomplished here is that I have given purpose to HER pain. I believe that by sharing this story, I can reach countless grown children who hold animosity towards their parents and show them that forgiveness is not only possible, it is liberating. I believe that for many years I thought my anger was punishing my parent, in truth I was hostage within my own mind. Even if my readers never learn the 'why' in their parent's addiction, they can realize that a root cause almost certainly exists and that by understanding THAT, perhaps a path to empathy, understanding and acceptance can be found.

One additional housekeeping note about this story and my writing process. Where possible, real names were used. If I was unable to obtain consent from people who are part of my life story, then I made up aliases. Additionally, conversations depicted may not necessarily be 100% accurate word for word, I did my best. Themes are all accurate and completely authentic.

1 in 4 children are currently living in a family with at least one parent addicted to drugs or alcohol. That is roughly 18.25 million children who need a voice. – nacoa.org

This is my story.

Matthew Whittington

Part 1

"He who cannot forgive breaks the bridge over which he himself must pass." - George Herbert

Chapter 1

On a sunny fall day in 1983 I was riding on the bench seat of an old Ford F-100 short box farm truck my dad had purchased from the farmer he was working for at the time. I was only 7 years old, my sister had just turned 2, and my little brother had just been born. I don't recall if the old truck had seat belts or not, but I do recall sitting next to the window not buckled in. At the time, it was the only vehicle my parents owned. On that particular day my mom needed the truck for some errands, so for lunch my dad came home and mom dropped him off at the farm after lunch.

Everything appeared normal to my dad as he was dropped off that afternoon. What he did not realize at the time was that my mom had been drinking. How much she'd had to drink, only she knew. The level of intoxication that day was sufficient enough to impair her judgement, and that afternoon as she sped through the Yakima Valley toward the farm to pick dad up from work, she lost control and rolled it in a field some farmers were working in. All three kids were tossed around the cab sustaining numerous cuts and bruises, my mom came through with no injuries.

That incident was the moment my dad became enlightened about the true nature of my mom's little secret. She was an alcoholic. My mom enjoyed drinking yet kept it a secret from him for many years. How she did this or why? I did not understand at the time, and the latter part of that question, why, would go on to vex me for over 35 years. Following that incident, my mom consented to inpatient treatment for the first time.

***

My parents, Frank and Janet Whittington, were married on October 20, 1973, almost eight full months after becoming engaged. My father has described my mom as being the popular girl in town; beautiful, kind and talented in sports she was involved in. Primary among those sports were swimming, diving and drill team though there were other things. My mom loved cars and was driving an Impala when she and my dad actually met for the first time. He claims she pulled up to his driver's door at a local Toppenish hangout, he was sitting at the wheel of a "muscled out '68 Camaro SS". The Camaro was a manual transmission and all my mom had ever driven was automatics, so my dad offered to teach her over a date. She refused at first but consented after he persisted.

Dad worked primarily as a farmer in the 1970's and early 80's, work that he enjoyed very much, yet paid very little. So you can imagine that after having three kids my folks had some decisions to make. Farming pay was not going to sustain for a family of five when there were little to no benefits to be had. Whether by persuasion or compulsion the decision was made to pick up and move the family to the West side of Washington State, where there were better jobs to be had and more opportunity.

My dad got on as a maintenance guy in the machine shop my Papa, Jack King, worked at. For the first year on the West side, we lived in the basement of my Papa and Nana's home. I went to second grade just up the street from there, all I remember about that school was learning for the first time how to throw a football during recess. As it turns out, I was actually better at catching it than throwing it. The second and final thing I remember was, my Papa was a drinker. He had a glass of liquor in his hands or sitting next to his recliner every single day.

Following that school year my parents got into, what I can only assume was, some government subsidized low income housing in North Everett. The unit we lived in was 2-3 blocks from Hawthorne Elementary School and I was able to walk there every day. After school, during breaks and summers I played outside quite a bit. I don't recall spending much time indoors, mainly because my mom's drinking had intensified so much that I just preferred playing in the streets with neighborhood kids. My dad worked very long hours and my mom had her hands full with two younger kids and figuring out how to hide her addiction. In fact, there were many times she'd write a note for me to buy her cigarettes at this convenient store about 6 blocks away, and they would sell me those cigarettes!

We lived in that North Everett spot for two years, and those were the first years I remember my parents fighting a lot. My dad worked so much, my mom drank so much and in the intersecting hours they fought so much it's not hyperbole to say I got away with roaming just about anywhere and nobody seemed to take much notice. If you've ever been in a community composed of primarily low income, government subsidized housing you know what kind of shit hole I'm talking about and the thought in retrospect is quite scary. Those streets were where I was first exposed to dirty magazines, the Playboy channel, littered liquor bottles and needles. It was not unusual for me to ride my BMX several blocks up to the major city strip and into different stores or up to the YMCA without telling my mom. Additionally, I would frequently visit four different neighborhood girls and two neighborhood boys, only one of which do I believe my parents had contact information for. One night some thug stole my BMX right off our porch. I was furious! I walked up and down every street in the neighborhood looking for it, and even walked as far as the waterfront which was about a mile to the West of where we lived. What I would have done had I spotted the bike? Who knows, but it's probably best that my parents collectively saw the writing on the wall and moved us the hell out of there. I was 10 years old.

Chapter 2

Dad managed to find a house for rent about 5 miles North of Arlington, Washington, about an hour North of Seattle. It was a four-bedroom, yellow rambler on about 5 acres and I wouldn't move again until I graduated high school. At first I was bummed to leave my friends behind, but my parents allowed me to keep one friendship alive and well for the rest of my years there with a boy named JD, I think to help ease the transition and also because he was a good-natured boy like myself that my parents had grown fond of. We often arranged overnight stays at each other's places. What was great about JD was that he didn't have an ideal home dynamic either, so we related well to each other. I didn't have to be embarrassed about my parents and specifically my mom, because his parents fought too. To this day if I call JD, even if it's been years since we last spoke, it's like we never spent a day apart.

The first friend I made in Arlington was the neighbor boy up the hill from the house, he was a year behind me in school; Chad Arnold. His parents were the ones renting the property to my parents. As often as possible I made sure that when we played, it was outside or at their house. I was embarrassed by my mom's drinking so much that I didn't want him to see it. Of course, Chad eventually figured it out and it became less of a big deal, we tended to just ignore her, placate her, or we'd just stay outside. Around this time I really started to pay much closer attention to the specifics of her addiction and changes in demeanor and behavior. My mom wasn't a mean drunk in the classical sense you think of, but she was certainly obnoxious and frank with her words. That filter sober people have, she didn't. So I can't say she was physically or even verbally abusive, but to me it was deeper, it was emotional. Further, in the formative mind of a fifth-grade youth, I felt it was personal. I rationalized in my young mind that she was trying to embarrass me and hurt my friendships. Of course in hindsight I know this is absurd, I didn't understand how alcohol changes behavior, but that was one of the first moments I recall resentment towards my mom.

An activity Chad was really into was baseball. I'd never had much interest in baseball before moving to Arlington, though my dad did. Dad was a good baseball player in his youth and even as recently as our days living in North Everett he had been involved in recreational softball leagues. Since Chad liked baseball, I decided to ask about playing little league with him. I fell in love with baseball when my parents got me onto the team, we're talking full immersion obsession with baseball, its history and strategy. Spring of 1987 was my first year and I had just watched the Mets win the World Series over the Red Sox, my favorite player to watch in that series was the Mets catcher, #8, Gary Carter. I asked the little league coach to play catcher and let me wear #8. He granted my wish, not because I was highly adept at the position, but nobody else wanted to play it. Chad ended up on the same team, which was fortunate because practice started before my dad got home, but not before my mom was already well and truly drunk. So, I rode with Chad in his mom's car to practice more often than not. I would find out later that Chad's parents forbade him from riding in a car my mom was driving under any circumstance, I would imagine they felt compelled to make sure I made it to practice safely as well.

My dad went to most of the games for the two years I was in little league, whereas my mom went to none. Truth be told, our teams weren't very good, we won maybe 4 games in two years. Dad was constantly standing behind the backstop, harassing umpires, he even got kicked out of a few games as a fan. Yes he was THAT dad. I'm sure some parents, some opponents and all the umpires couldn't stand him.

My teammates loved my dad for it, and nobody loved my dad behind that backstop more than I did. The way I saw it, he had our backs. If he cared enough to be so involved that umpires wanted him out of the game, it made me work that much harder to be the best ballplayer I could be.

Dad worked long hours and still chose to dedicate his spare hours being a terrific parent and role model instead of an alcoholic like mom. Meanwhile, my mom was well into a twelve pack by the time we got home. I'm sure there was some justification she gave for absence; she had to stay home with my siblings, work on dinner, do laundry, etc. I called bull-crap on all of that, everyone else had moms there with younger kids running around behind the dugouts.

We lived maybe a mile from our home field, my thought at the time was, she could at least come to the home games. In my mind then, and for years to come, she made a choice between drinking and watching her son play a game he loved. Drinking won. Little league was the turning point, it was her apathy over my interest in baseball that caused me to start hating my mom. I resented her for decades over it.

Chapter 3

Middle school was a total nightmare. I suppose to put it more accurately middle school years were *my* nightmare. You see, by the time I was old enough for middle school, I was also old enough and aware enough to have a deeper awareness of my environments. I began to understand more clearly what my parents actually fought about.

They fought about money a lot and one of the primary triggers of this particular fight was how much my mom spent to stay drunk. I'm not sure if it was during middle school or not, but at some point my mom must have overdrawn the account or spent money my dad had saved because there was a big screaming match about it. My siblings and I would just look at each other and be uncomfortable when these fights happened.

During this particular fight there was name calling. My dad would call mom "Jack", presumably because she was drunk, like her father Jack. My mom called my dad "Florence", presumably because he's a stubborn ass, like his mother Florence. The whole thing was totally stupid, disrespectful and quite frankly an exceedingly poor example to your kids on how to be a loving spouse. The resolution to that particular fight was separate accounts and me vowing to myself that I would never drink alcohol or yell at my future wife.

The real legacy of those middle school years I would say are isolation and independence.

For starters if I wanted to go anywhere away from the house, it had to be somewhere the neighbor was going so I could ride with his mom, or my dad would have to be home from work to take me. Neither scenario occurred often since we lived 5 miles out of town. As a result, if Chad wasn't available to play catch, shoot hoops, or play out in the woods, then I would be all on my own.

Some common activities included riding my three-wheeler through the acres of trees, or out to Pilchuck Creek about half a mile to the North. I would listen to Seattle Mariners games on the radio if the weather was bad outside, occasionally I would keep a scorecard for the game. I enjoyed building airplane models for dad to hang from my bedroom ceiling. I found an old TV and Atari at a yard sale one spring and managed to scrounge enough money to pick those up. A lifelong passion for gaming was born that day. Common among all of these activities and dozens of others I put into action, they worked to isolate and distance myself from my mom and her addiction. I did manage to make it to one middle school dance, just one. At that dance my future wife asked me to dance, I said no.

Some people may think, 'Hey that's great you were able to do all those things and become so independent'. Or you may wonder, 'What's so awful about all that?' Maybe you're reading this and thinking to yourself I'm a whiny complainer who ought to be thankful for the roof over my head and food in my belly.

Truth be told, it was totally depressing as an early teen to be so isolated and stunted in my growth as a person. Where was I learning my social skills? Where was I learning to communicate with girls? At the aforementioned dance I didn't just say no to my future wife, I stood next to the wall and engaged with nobody. Girls terrified me. I ended up a socially awkward introvert.

Other issues arise and compound when your dad leaves for work in the early morning, comes home late afternoon and your mom is already well buzzed when you step off the school bus. For starters, there was no help to be had with middle school curriculum homework. I recall asking each parent maybe once for help with homework. My dad said he didn't know how to do what I wanted help with, and I couldn't stomach the stench of cheap beer on my mom's breath. Another blown chance mom, thanks for nothing, never mind. Go back to your beer.

A second point of contention was an assumption on the part of my mom that I was old enough and responsible enough to keep an eye on my younger siblings. I was still a child myself! I wasn't qualified nor did I want to be their moral and ethical compass just so she could drink her ass off guilt free. Sure she kept them fed and clothed, but if I was home it was expected I would help watch them. How did I respond to this you might ask? With anger. I was mean to them. I frequently bullied them or blackmailed them into behaving rather than being a good big brother. I was especially brutal to my sister. She was willful and defiant, additionally it appeared she did not respect my 'authority.' So, I would put her in submission holds learned from rented VHS tapes depicting WWF stars in WrestleMania or Royal Rumble. My sister Sarah was stubborn and I was ruthless. It has taken decades for us to arrive at a place of mutual respect. I deeply regret my role in that relationship, though I was placed in an awful position I did not want nor deserve.

I got up in the mornings all on my own to get ready for school and walk myself to the bus stop. No parents there to make sure I had breakfast or drive me to the bus stop to sit in a warm car on rainy days. Dad was already at work and mom was hung over, sleeping it off. I never blamed my dad for that, he was the one working those long hours to keep the family above water. I hated my mom for being too drunk to get out of bed and you know, actually do mom things. I'd stood out there along the highway in the rain and would see how many rocks I could throw into our mailbox across the road. Chad would stand there next to me and compete to see who could get more rocks into the mailbox. Chad always had the better arm and control, I couldn't even have the satisfaction of landing more rocks in my parents' mailbox.

By middle school they had band you could get involved in. I loved music and wanted to play trumpet, saxophone or drums. My dad said no to all the above, we couldn't afford instrument rental. We sure could afford a twelve pack a night though. I got into the next best thing, choir. My singing voice wasn't particularly good, but at least there were lots of girls in the class, all of whom I was too terrified to talk to.

One particular time I remember coming home and mom was drunker than normal. I'd had a tough day at school or something and was fed up with my mom's crap. I confronted her. I told her she was a lousy drunk and told her how mad I was that she wasn't a regular mom. The answer I got back blew my mind. My mom looked me straight in the face and through slurred stuttering words said, "I don't know what you're talking about, I'm not drunk, I don't drink." Then she walked away leaning on the wall for balance as she did so.

Fury, pure fury. An outright bold face lie, right to my face. You don't lie to the people you love, guess she doesn't love me. So be it.

I went to the refrigerator and grabbed her open twelve pack of Schmidt's animal beer, then stormed out into the back yard. One by one, with my best outfielder throw, I hurled those unopened cans of beer deep into the woods and surrounding blackberry bushes. Words cannot describe the satisfaction I felt that day, knowing that she couldn't confront me over it. After all, if she said anything to me, it's an admission of guilt over her lies. The next day there was a fresh unopened twelve pack of Schmidt's when I got home from school, all twelve were direct deposited into the bushes promptly. I'm talking fresh from the store, unopened fresh brewed premium horse piss beer. For all I cared Bigfoot could drink them, because mom sure wasn't. The anger on her face was amusing to me, she knew I had her. Mom knew that if she said anything, it would mean an admission of her addiction.

I've always wondered what went through my mom's mind regarding my beer can chucking chess match with her. What I know for certain about my mom, she was one hell of a stubborn woman. An oddly defiant strength. I would imagine that a high percentage of parents would have turned that showdown into an education opportunity with their young teen. Maybe a chance to sit and have a heart to heart chat about what she was and why she was should have been in order. That wasn't my mom though. Nobody isolated themselves better than my mom, hell that's probably where I learned it.

What I do know for certain, her strategy changed. If she was in denial when this all started, she went full black ops secret underground alcoholism after that. She started hiding her stash and diversifying her alcohol portfolio. She started hiding cans of beer in all kinds of weird places. If it weren't the truth of my childhood the whole scene probably would have been funny. Chad found a few cans under the kitchen sink once when we were rinsing some dishes. I was astonished, under the sink! I mean it's warm under there, why would she keep her beer warm and still drink it? I found cans behind plates and bowls in the cupboards. I found beer under the bathroom sink. I found them in coat closets, in the china cabinet, in a laundry basket and even in the damn toilet reservoir a few times! Every single can I found went directly to the blackberry bushes, and she never gave me the satisfaction of saying a word about it to me. Then one day my dad came up to me and asked, "Matthew, are you throwing your mom's beer out into the woods?" My head dropped as I told him, "Yes." Dad just chuckled and told me to stop doing it, I did.

Funny thing about that level of denial was the aftermath of all the consumed beer. If dad wasn't drinking, and mom wasn't drinking, how in the hell could dozens of lawn bags of empty beer cans stack up around the back porch? I'm not talking kitchen bags, 55-gallon lawn bags! By the dozens. I asked her once to explain dozens of lawn bags of empty beer cans, she just denied that it was her drinking. I supposed at the time she just had me sized up as some gullible idiot.

Chapter 4

No child has perfect parents. No child. Parents are people and people make mistakes. I remember pitying my father for his position. I was a middle school teenage boy who pitied his father. I pitied him for being stuck in a situation with a hopeless alcoholic who had no desire to get meaningful help. I never pitied my mother. Never. I didn't understand addiction, how could I? In my mind, drinking beer was a choice. My dad chose not to. In my mind, she was selfishly putting her desire to be a lousy drunk above all else in life, above her husband and kids.

During some of their fights my dad would get so angry and frustrated that he would get in his car and drive off. Where he went? We had no idea. I just know that he got in his car and left us all alone with Janet the drunk. It scared the hell out of me when he would do that. I wondered each and every time if he was coming back. I thought to myself at the time, 'Man I wish that was me driving away. I would never come back.' Part of me wanted him to be happy and maybe he could only find happiness by giving up and leaving us behind with her. So I came to hate my mom for that. I hated her for causing him all that frustration and not allowing him the family he wanted when they married.

Dad of course returned every time he left. Sometimes he'd return and all would be quiet, sometimes he'd return for more fighting. Either way he returned, to my relief. I didn't want to be left alone with her. Oddly, it made me love and respect my dad all the more. He wouldn't leave us behind to deal with that nightmare.

I worked my butt off in middle school to get straight A's. I never quite achieved a 4.0 in middle school, though I was regularly close. It was satisfying to be awesome at something without the help of my parents. In truth I got those grades in spite of them. I don't recall ever throwing it in their faces in the sense of, 'Look what I did without you.' Though deep down I thought it. Even so, it was cool to get my dad's praise for the grades. He said a few times that I must have gotten my knack of academics from my mom. She did tell me a number of times to be a good speller, 'or everyone will think you are stupid.' I give her credit for that advice, I always have. Though the truth is, she didn't work on spelling with me, I worked my ass off. I didn't argue with my dad about my mom's role regarding my intelligence, but I thought he was wrong. I thought to myself, she doesn't help me with a damn thing, all she teaches me is what a mom shouldn't be.

We got awards in middle school for two things: grades and attendance. Regarding the attendance, I didn't miss a single day of middle school. I was the Cal Ripken Jr of Post Middle School. I just didn't miss school, fact is I preferred the awkward outsider feel of school over being stuck at home with my mom.

The best memories of middle school years weren't middle school. My favorite memory of middle school was baseball. If I wasn't playing catch with Chad, I was begging my dad to hit me fly balls and grounders after work and on weekends. Dad could never hit me enough balls. I could run down pop ups for hours in our backyard. He'd wear a glove on his left hand to catch the ones I threw back to him and a baseball bat in his right. We'd only stop when we ran out of baseballs hit or thrown into blackberry bushes.

By the end of middle school Chad and I got onto a city ball team together, the Arlington Royals. Chad was our best starting pitcher, by far. I on the other hand played third base and left field. The coach started me every game, and I hit .400 that year. I was by far the fastest kid on the team so the coach taught me to drag bunt and he had me lead off. I was always on base, and if I got to first base, there was no signal the coach could give to have me not steal bases. If I got to first base, I'd have third base stolen in no more than two pitches. They couldn't throw me out. In sixteen games I stole 30 bases. During one particular home game an opposing player hit a ball so far, it was clear he'd make it home before the throw came in, there were no fences so that ball just kept rolling. I was playing third base that game, I knew it was a homerun so rather than stand in the batter's way, I stood well into foul territory, past the third base coach's box. That kid rounded the third base bag very wide with his forearm up to run me over. The collision was so nasty that the coach had to pull me from the game. I'm fairly certain that I was concussed and I know I was bleeding. My dad completely lost his mind screaming at the umpire to throw that kid who flattened me out of the game, after all, that forearm shiver was grossly blatant. The only person to get thrown out though, was dad. I played the best defense of my life, made the All-Star team, and our team finished the year in first place. Mom never saw me play the best baseball of my life.

The following season Chad and I played on another city ball team, Northwest Hardwoods. I led off that season too. The coach had me play mostly left field all season and was even trying to teach me to be a switch hitter. I spent hours in the cages learning to hit balls left handed. I had more power left handed but made a lot less contact. About midway through the season he put me at leadoff and told me to try hitting lefty. On the first pitch thrown to me I hit the ball over the fence, but foul. I went on to walk in that at bat and stole two bases. Next at bat, I struck out on three pitches and thus ended my lefty hitting experiment.

Several games after my switch-hitting experiment the coach started me at third base. During that game I took a tough grounder bounce to my nose and it broke. I bled a lot, and then I spent the rest of the season back in the outfield.

I tell these stories of tough bounces and head injuries for a reason. By the time I got home from all these games, my mom was looking at buzzed in her rear-view mirror, she was totally drunk. Too drunk to attend my injuries. All the medical care I got was what I gave myself, bags of ice.

Later that year, in the summer, I was riding my three-wheeler through a nearby field of tall grass. Now, I never wrecked my three-wheeler. My dad had taught me that three-wheelers are only dangerous when you're reckless. I was a cautious and technically sound rider when it came to that machine. Yet, on this particular summer day I was speeding through this field and the right tire found a log I had missed. I tipped over to the left and the left rear tire ran over my upper left thigh, slicing it open down to the white stuff. The injury didn't bleed as much as I would have thought, but it was a deep wound about 5 inches long. I managed to get back on the three-wheeler and got it started in order to get home. Upon getting home I reported the injury to my mom. She was too drunk to get me somewhere for stitches. Her solution was to wash it out and tape it back together. I still have a nasty scar there.

Chapter 5

During one of the summers in middle school a friend and his grandpa invited me to tag along on a multi week trip up over Snoqualmie Pass in the mountains of Washington to stay there on a ranch while his grandpa worked on building a retirement cabin. Excitedly I packed for the trip, it was a great opportunity to get away from my parents fights over alcoholism. Visions of trout fishing and ATV's filled my head, it was going to be a modern Huck Finn experience!

On the way over I got to ride in the back of a pickup truck since it had a canopy. The other boy and I drank sodas and ate gas station junk food during the nearly four-hour trip. I would learn years later that the trip could be made faster, but his grandpa took mostly back roads from Arlington to the foothills below Snoqualmie Pass. During the climb up we stopped for burgers and an old-fashioned milkshake somewhere along the way. In my mind I remember it being an all-around great start to an exciting trip.

Upon arriving I noticed a few things. First, there was an old, World War 2 era jeep sitting there. Second, the cabin was in the early stages of construction, still in framing if I recall correctly. Finally third, there was an old RV on the premises there during construction where we would all be staying. As I understood it my friend and I would have to share the fold out while his grandpa had the bedroom.

As a person may imagine with young middle school aged boys, the first thing we asked to do was drive the jeep. The jeep of course, was a manual transmission and I couldn't quite figure it out. My friend however, had been taught some basics, at least enough to slowly ramble around the ranch. The jeep was geared for high torque, so as it was, there was not much danger of the two of us reaching high speeds. My buddy did the driving and I stood up in the back as if I was operating a .50 cal. It was a blast, for a while.

The two of us puttered around the property like some dynamic Special Forces strike team for a bit, meanwhile his grandpa got in some work on the cabin and chores around the property. As the day wound down, my friend's grandpa stepped out front of the would be cabin and picked up a garden hose. We drove by as if to strafe him, and the hose got turned on us. My buddy went to make a hasty retreat and jerked his foot off the clutch and onto the gas too fast, the jeep lurched, and I was thrown in the air.

Foggy recollection number one, bright light. I remember bright light. I, in fact, distinctly remember blinding white light. There was yelling and blurred figures moving about my body and some flashing lights.

Foggy recollection number two, paramedics. I remember being in an ambulance and a paramedic looking down at me. I cannot remember what the paramedic specifically looked like or even simple details such as whether or not the medic was a man or woman. I don't remember what was said or where they took me. In fact, I have no memory at all of arriving at a hospital, staying at a hospital or even leaving a hospital. To this day I cannot say if I was admitted for any length of time, though I'm inclined to say that I was not.

The first semi solid memory I have of the incident was of pulling up to the RV back on the ranch and led to sitting at the little dining table inside. I remember vaguely at some point my parents were called and told what had happened. The call may have been made from the hospital or it may have been made from the ranch. Bottom line, the call was made, my dad offered to come and pick me up. I had said I wanted to stay. I remember that I didn't want my dad to have to make that trip, and that I convinced him I was ok. I wish he had ignored me.

My friend and his grandpa went on to fill me in on all the details about what had transpired. When I flew from the jeep, it was straight backwards. It was as if the jeep had just taken off and my body stayed right where it was briefly. Somehow my feet must have clipped something in the jeep, as it was described to me my feet flew up to the point where my body was nearly parallel to the ground. In the ensuing showdown with gravity, my thick head lost and hence hit the ground first. I was knocked unconscious immediately.

During the subsequent chaos and call for an ambulance, they said I regained consciousness, somewhat. The way it was described to me, I woke up enough to ramble about lights. Lights were the only coherent thing I uttered, I've been told the rest was senseless babbling. The doctors diagnosed me with a severe concussion, and I was in a fair amount of pain.

Within a day or two of the incident, I noticed adult magazines in a drawer in the bathroom. Magazines like Penthouse, Penthouse Forum and Hustler right there within reach for young boys just starting puberty. I, of course, was very interested. I read the letters and flipped through all of it. Later that night, my friend and I were taught card games by his grandpa and he made us drinks with liquors such as peppermint schnapps and Everclear. I was 13 years old. For the purposes of full disclosure, I rather liked the taste of peppermint schnapps. The Everclear was obscenely strong, however. Before long I began to realize my head hurt less.

As we sat there playing cards, blackjack if memory serves, the old man put his hand on my thigh and asked how I liked his magazines. My head swam in the fog of the liquor and I told him that I liked them very much. He followed up and asked me such questions as; what I liked best and did I have any questions. It made me very uncomfortable so I just told him that I was very tired. In reflection I have found it to be very odd that my friend's grandpa was comfortable talking to me in front of his grandson like that.

I went and laid down in the bed since my friend still wanted to play with his grandpa. Sometime later I felt the old man lay down next to me. The man backed up to my body and tried to rub my genitals to arousal. I wouldn't say that the response is what he was hoping for, yet the effort was still made to pull my penis through the fly of my shorts and he attempted to insert it into his rectum. I just turned over as if he had just agitated me in my sleep, at that he finally left me alone. For that night anyway.

Some version of this charade went on for the rest of the trip. The man was never successful at achieving insertion, but it was not for lack of effort. He tried to persuade me with magazines, flattery, and activities such as letting me drive his pickup down the road. It all failed. When it was time to go home, I was very relieved. While I was accustomed to the psychological and emotional toll alcoholism exacted on me, this attempted sexual abuse was next level stuff. I had no idea how to deal with it and no desire to talk about it.

I told my parents nothing.

***

Some time passed by, maybe months or even as much as a year. The police department in Everett, Washington contacted my parents. They wanted to interview me about this man. Another child had come forward about abuse. Bravo to that kid for his bravery, Lord knows it wasn't me. The police became aware somehow that I was a potential victim, that was how my parents found out. My dad took me to a location the police indicated would work for their interview, I think it was actually a house in North Everett. Police detectives did some talking with the adults in the room, then interviewed me one on one. I told them everything, all the details. I remember my dad being furious. What conversations he had with the authorities, I was not privy to, nor have I ever been enlightened since. The ultimate conclusion of this interview and charges brought on my friend's grandpa were as follows:

1. I adamantly refused the desire of prosecutors to testify in court. At that point I was done, I'd lived it enough. The police threatened that I may be put under subpoena, it never happened.
2. My parents, specifically my dad probed about how I was doing and whether or not I wanted counseling. I told them no, I was done talking.
3. The man went to prison.

This entire chapter of my life has a very important connection to my mother, specifically relating to her pain and the genesis of her addiction. An opportunity existed in that moment to change the course of history, had my mother only seized it. Unfortunately, she chose differently. I would not discover until decades later just how close we were to reconciliation.

Chapter 6

All my life I've been enraptured by flight. Surely a psychologist could sit down with me to break down all the underlying reasons why I'm drawn to slip the bonds of gravity. Since I was little there is one dream I have over and over. The details vary in the dream, but the mechanics are the same; in my dreams I can literally extend my arms for powered flight and gliding. I can dive for inertia only to soar for higher reaches. Waking from these dreams is always a disappointment. If you are among the folks who subscribe to reincarnation theories, maybe it means I've been some bird of prey in a past life or perhaps the future. Religious conversations aside, I believe the dream is my heart's desire. I was meant to fly.

As a young child in the Yakima Valley, my eyes traced the graceful dance of crop dusters. Living in Everett, Washington, home of Boeing's largest plant, the planes became super-sized. There were also nearby military installations to consider; Naval Air Station Whidbey Island and McChord Air Force Base chief among them. By the sixth grade I could identify aircraft far overhead by silhouette with exceeding accuracy. My obsession was fed by a combination of model airplane constructions which my dad hung from my bedroom ceiling with fishing line, dragging my dad to every airshow within driving distance and the Top Gun / Iron Eagle films so popular in my generational culture.

My mind was made up. I had no desire to be a doctor, lawyer, teacher or firefighter. I wanted to be a fighter pilot. Back then my mind saw only a handful of options; F/A-18s, F-15s, F-14s or F-16s. That's what it was all about, I wanted to own the sky. All I had to do was figure out how to get where I wanted to go.

Airshows, that's why I would drag my dad to all those airshows. We'd get up very early in the morning on airshow days, 4:30-5:00 am wakeup. Dad would pack a cooler with sandwiches and soda and off we'd go to Paine Field, Everett, Washington. The cool thing about those airshows at Paine Field was all the grass parking so close to show center. We'd be one of the first vehicles in line when the gates opened for admission and dad would get as close to the flight line as he could. He'd park with the tailgate to flight line and we'd setup the lawn chairs and cooler for a show that was many hours away from starting. Dad would throw me a little money, enough for a program and one or two souvenirs and then off we'd go.

At first he'd walk around with me to check out all the static display aircraft. Program in hand, I'd walk up to every aircraft, identify it for him, then get the aircraft's crew and ground crew to sign my program in the appropriate place. I'd ask the crews all I could about the aircraft and tell them all I knew. Some were entertained and engaging, some were a little more gruff and begrudging. One great example of an engaging crew would be a British Nimrod crew. They were very friendly, helpful, and seemed to be having a good time themselves. That particular crew even setup a rope around a blank area of grass only to hang a sign that said, "Stealth Fighter." Of course in the late 80s, the existence of the F-117 Stealth Fighter was still parts, urban legend, black ops, and speculation. I just remember the humor of their "Stealth Fighter" to be exceedingly clever, and I also found it funny to call them the "Nimrod Crew".

Inevitably Dad would get tired. We'd walk back to the truck to eat a sandwich and drink some soda. Then he'd ask me if I could remember how to get back to where we parked. Of course I could, I was an expert airshow land navigator. Once dad was convinced of my bearings, he'd cut me loose to fly solo around the flight deck to gather autographs and take in all the wonders of the aircraft. All of the airplanes and helicopters were wonderful, yet the military airframes held special places in my heart. If it was a fighter plane, I'd stand there and talk that pilot's ear off. One F-16 pilot in particular was especially helpful. He told me, "Son get good grades, don't slack off in school. Stay out of trouble. Get your degree, you'll need a degree to fly." Then he signed a picture of an F-16 in a straight up vertical climb with the words, 'Blue Skies.' I still have it.

Finally, after hours of walking up and down the flight line the show would start. I'd work my way back to dad before the big acts kicked off, usually by the time military jets took off for their routines. Most years the show culminated with either the Air Force Thunderbirds or Navy Blue Angels. Those teams were IT. Those pilots were elite, my idols. To get to the cockpit of one of those planes; to be a Thunderbird or Blue Angel would be the ultimate dream come true, my Everest.

Of course every great show came to an end. With it, the end of something I would look forward to all year long, like Christmas. Then we'd have to go home, exhausted and fulfilled. Truly great days that I cherished and clung to for ultimate fond memories, only to be tempered with frustration and contempt upon arriving home to a mom too drunk to engage with. Too drunk to share my passion with. Too drunk to share my dreams with. Too drunk to share my life with. I knew what I wanted to be and how to get there, all I had to do was survive her addiction and find a way to get into college. Should be easy, just had to keep up the hard work and ace high school with no help on the home front.

Chapter 7

I embarked on my freshman year of high school in September of 1990 at Arlington High School. On day one all classes and choices were made with one goal in mind, building my college resume. Among the classes I signed up for were the highest level of math I could test into, history, English, chemistry and first year Japanese. Most freshman, if they take a foreign language at all, usually go for Spanish. I reasoned at the time that while Spanish may be a little easier to learn, that Japanese was worldlier in the modern economy and had a higher degree of difficulty.

For the first time in my life I also played organized football. The high school had a freshman team, so I talked my mom and dad into letting me try. Dad took more convincing, I think he was concerned that I was too small to play high school football. Back then I weighed about 130 pounds, maybe I was a little small. During the first days, coaches had me play cornerback on defense and wingback on offense. It's tough to get a real feel for how good I really was at football. The offense only ever seemed to call running plays, I only broke up a few passes. On offense I didn't get the ball much, I was mostly a decoy. I only ever saw real game action at kick returner. I'd never even played kick returner in practice, the first time I ever returned a kick was in real game action.

Dad really disliked that I played football, so I quit the team. Quitting that team was a decision I've always regretted.

Sophomore year of high school mom helped me get a part time job at the Chevron gas station. Mom had a job out at this Chevron as a cashier. Back in 1991 this particular Chevron still had full service pumps and a propane filling area. The guy who owned the place needed a few younger people to run out and pump gas, fill propane, wash windshields, etc. Other tasks I took on to fill time and keep busy were such little things as stocking and cleaning. Before long the owner really came to like my work ethic and reliability. I managed to help get a few of my buddies jobs out there, thanks in part to the credibility I'd earned through hard work.

One day I came in and the owner pulled me back to his office. I was informed that he'd had to fire my mom earlier that day, she had been drinking store inventory while back in the cooler stocking it. He explained his reasoning to me and asked me to not be upset, the termination was necessary. Furthermore, he mainly seemed worried that I would quit because he had fired my mom. Truth is, I was incredibly embarrassed and angry. The severity of her addiction seemed to be growing, I mean theft?! I was ashamed of what she was. This conversation I was forced to have with the station owner should not have even been necessary. Apparently, it wasn't enough for her to have this awful habit in the privacy of our own home. Of course I stayed on.

Besides the part time job and focused academics, I played baseball for the high school too. Though with less time to practice in the offseason with my dad and friends, my skills dulled a little. I never made varsity during freshman - junior years.

As high school went on I continued to take increasingly difficult classes. Among the classes I took were AP English

(3 times), physics, advanced mathematics such as calculus/statistics and computer science. I did however forego second year Japanese. During the conversation with the counselor I said, "When will I ever go to Japan?"

Before sophomore year, I took driver's education at the high school. One particular day, mom was supposed to pick me up after class, she never showed up. I went to the school office to call home and nobody answered. So, I walked home. It was summer and the walk was about five miles, mostly along a two lane highway. I was so pissed. By the time I got home my mom was well and truly drunk. As angry as I was that she'd forgotten to come and get me or answer the phone, I was infuriated that she didn't even apologize. That particular event stood out in my mind for years as proof that she truly didn't have family set as her life priority.

Chapter 8

During junior year high school I was within the top 5 academically every quarter. I never saw a grade on any paper lower than A-. Junior year was the year I started attending college fairs, talking to representatives from numerous universities, and was narrowing down where I wanted to go. In state colleges that I corresponded most frequently with were Seattle Pacific University, Gonzaga and Western Washington University. I was also in contact with a handful of out of state schools, to include Pepperdine and Dartmouth.

I didn't know exactly where I wanted to go. What was certain in my mind, the further away from the alcoholism the better. My mom was getting worse with each passing year it seemed. I don't know exactly how much alcohol she consumed on a nightly basis, but I do know that the amount was significant. Fights between my parents were a nightly event. Dozens of lawn bags full of crushed cans stacked up on the side of the house. I'm sure the financial strain of her addiction was particularly tough on my dad, and that fact combined with two more failed attempts at inpatient treatment had to be frustrating and maddening. The fact is, she didn't want to be sober. My mom had no desire for sobriety, and seemingly in my eyes no desire to be a functioning mother. One time in particular I screamed in frustration at her, "WHY IS BEING A DRUNK MORE IMPORTANT TO YOU THAN US?!" Her answer was a simple cop out, "I'm my father's daughter."

***

Years earlier in school I had done a historical project for the school culture fair, my family history in the United States Military. My dad's father was an Army veteran of World War 2. I knew very little about him since he had died when my dad was a teen. My dad served in the Army, 101st Airborne in Vietnam. My Papa served in the Navy, specifically Pacific Theater, World War 2 as an airframe mechanic aboard the USS Ommaney Bay.

Early in 1945, shortly after transiting the Surigao Strait into the Sulu Sea, a twin-engine Japanese suicide plane penetrated the fleet undetected and headed for the Ommaney Bay. The plane clipped the island and crashed into the flight deck on the forward starboard side. Bombs carried by the plane released; one penetrated the flight deck and detonated below, setting off a series of explosions among fully fueled planes on the hangar deck. The second bomb passed through the hangar deck, ruptured the fire main on the second deck then exploded.

Forward water pressure, power and bridge communications were all immediately lost. The ensuing inferno and thick black smoke quickly made it impossible to fight the fires. Escort ships were not able to lend power to the fight due to exploding ammunition, incredible heat, and stored torpedo warheads that command thought to be in imminent danger of exploding as well. The order to abandon ship was given at 1750. At 1945 the carrier was sunk by a torpedo from the USS Burns. In total 95 sailors lost their lives, my Papa had to swim for his life since rescue boats were unable to navigate too close to the sinking ship.

Papa talked a great deal to me and others about his fellow Ommaney Bay survivors. It was clear to me that despite the tragedy and loss, he was quite close with those men, even 50 years later.

***

The preceding historical anecdote is critical for so much in the context of how and why I made the decisions I made during my junior year. As I wrote earlier, the desire was already a driving force in my life to become a fighter pilot. Now, you could point to the influence of Top Gun, watching the Blue Angels once or twice a year in Western Washington, or consider the cultural mood following the events of Desert Storm and the fact that one of my cousins was an ordnance man aboard a carrier. Whatever it was, most likely a confluence of all the above, I had decided I wanted to fly Hornets in the Navy. I had asked my dad for help financially to submit college applications, he had told me that not only could the family not afford the cost of simply submitting applications, we could not afford application fees for scholarships, and we could definitely not afford tuition. Especially out of state tuition. I was running out of options. Despair was setting in. I felt like I had completely wasted years of hard academic school work, total futility.

The resentment I felt toward my parents and especially the vitriolic disdain I harbored over my mom were reaching a boiling point. How was it right that the selfish addiction of one parent could utterly stun the growth of my lifelong career path? There had to be a solution. I would escape this hell, somehow, I had to get out.

A solution presented itself not long after my dad had all but told me that I was on my own to figure it out. For the past several months dad and I had, what I can only generously refer to as, a semiprofessional lawn maintenance company. Really my dad had found a way to obtain a few self-propelled walk-behind lawn mowers, one rider, some trimming equipment and a trailer. (The irony was not lost on me, even then, that the money spent on this small business experiment was more than enough to pay some application and scholarship fees at universities, but I digress.) I think we had less than five yards. One of them was Papa's. On this particular day we had just finished cutting Papa's yard, and by we I mean I had just finished cutting his yard. Nana had made me a peanut butter and grape jelly sandwich with apple juice, and I sat down at the dining room table to eat. Papa sat next to me and asked, "Matthew, your graduation will be here before you know it, what are your plans?" I told him that I wanted to get into the Naval Academy and fly Hornets off of carriers.

Upon laying my plan out before him I had expected him to beam with pride and offer words of encouragement. I didn't exactly get the response I had expected. He wasn't dismissive or discouraging, rather he just nodded his head and said, "That would be a fine choice and the Navy would be good for you, but why not the Marines?"

The Marines?

Frankly I had given no consideration to the Marine Corps until this point.

I was confused. I asked, "Papa, all you ever talk about is the Navy. Why the Marines?"

His response was simple, yet I will not forget the impact and profound simplicity of his answer for the rest of my life. Papa just matter-of-factly said, "Matthew, I've watched you be prideful and strive for perfection in everything you do. Your academics, baseball, even the work you've done. Nobody is more prideful, nobody does it better than the Marines."

Sold!

Chapter 9

The Marines.

I got in my car on a Saturday morning toward the end of junior year and decided that talking to a Marine recruiter was the next logical step. I didn't tell my parents where I was going, I just left.

Many thoughts occupied the mind as I drove my 1974 Oldsmobile Omega toward the Marine recruiting office in South Everett. First, the commercials, *The Few, The Proud, the Marines.* What the hell did that even mean? Did it mean that they try to flunk everybody out? Could I be a fighter pilot in the Marines? Papa said I could, yet all I ever thought of when somebody said Marines, was on the ground warfighters. I had no idea where the nearest Marine base even was! That had to mean it was far away from home, maybe that wasn't such a bad thing.

I pulled up to the recruiting station and noticed another branch had an office right next door to the Marines. In fact, one of their recruiters was standing outside and tried to lure me in the door, I smiled and told the guy, no thanks. As I walked into the Marine office, a few looked up and acknowledged that I had walked in, yet none seemed to be in a big rush to come greet me. In hindsight I've wondered if that was some tactic. You know, like feign interest to seem mysterious and desirable or something. I digress, after a few moments a Sergeant stood up and greeted me, his name was Sergeant Parker. After chatting for a few minutes he asked if I knew what I wanted to do. I told him fighter pilot. He nodded and asked if I had a degree, I of course had to admit that I did not.

Admittedly, I don't recall the exact specifics of what was said. What I can recall is that after discerning that I lacked a degree, the talk turned to the ROTC program, Sergeant Parker admitted he could walk me through and help out with the application process. The Sergeant indicated that often times applicants are not accepted on the first try and that it was standard practice for folks to enlist in the Marine Corps and continue to try. At that point he asked how I felt about taking the ASVAB. ASVAB tests were used during that time period and may still be used now to evaluate your overall level of intelligence and certain scores could open up more desirable jobs, or MOS assignments. I felt pretty confident that I could score well on his test so I consented to take it right then.

I don't specifically remember what was on the test besides some spatial reasoning stuff. Suffice to say I performed well enough. Sergeant Parker indicated I scored well enough to pick just about anything I wanted to do, so I told him to sign me on as an airframe mechanic. I figured if it was good for my Papa, then I could do it too. Besides, the job would get me up close to the aircraft I wanted to fly.

There were just two small problems.

For starters, I still had a full year of high school to complete. Dropping out was not a consideration for many reasons, chief among them; without a diploma I wouldn't get the job I wanted in the Corps, I still had sights set on ROTC, and most importantly I just didn't want to. As much as I hated going home every day to a drunk and parents constantly at each other's throats, the work had been put in and quitting would be wasteful.

The issue concerning Sergeant Parker more, was my age. I was still just 17. I couldn't do an early enlistment without the consent of my parents. Sergeant Parker told me that if we could get my parents to agree and sign, he could get me a one-year delayed entry contract complete with choice of duty station coast and guaranteed promotion out of basic training. In return I had to give the Marines six years active duty instead of four. The years didn't concern me since in my mind I would be getting into ROTC anyway. Getting my parents to sign off on the Marine Corps though, that I wasn't certain about.

Within a week I had arranged for the recruiter to drive out to the house in Arlington so he could talk to my parents. I remember them being very reticent about signing off on my enlistment. Dad in particular was melancholy, and I would think very concerned that I appeared to be giving up on my dreams. Sergeant Parker and I both told my parents that the door to ROTC was not slammed shut, that I would get invaluable experience and tools as an enlisted Marine should the ROTC program not accept me right away. Reluctantly they signed. It was done. The day was June 26, 1993, and in one year I would be departing for Marine Corps Basic Training or off to college in ROTC.

Through the summer of 1993 I began to notice long time friendships start to crack a little. It is amazing how perceptive people can be at a young age. As if most of the people close to me knew what was coming, they distanced themselves. In a year I would be gone, why stay attached? So, I volunteered to work near full time over the summer.

When I wasn't working, I did a drive around the state with one of my childhood buddies and some camping in the mountains. As the final year of school approached, senior year, I did something totally stupid. With the exception of AP English, I only signed up for easy classes. In place of advanced math, I took accounting. In place of getting the second year of foreign language, I took weight training. Fact is, I saw no point in busting my ass when it appeared I may or may not get into college. Besides the weight training would only help for Marine training, right?

Another activity I was involved in on a regular basis over the summer and early school year was recruiting office pool functions. A pool function with recruiters is like reserve duty, lite. Some examples of pool functions would be fitness tests, flag football and weapons familiarization.

Furthermore, the time period immediately after my enlistment felt like a period of erosion between mom and me. What confused me and angered me more was the fact that she seemed so happy about it. Granted the enlistment was my idea and I did want it, but for the purpose of getting out of there. Every letter I received from Dartmouth or Pepperdine only flamed my resentment more. That was the path I was meant to follow! Not this roundabout way of getting where I wanted to go. Jumping through all these other hoops and still not possibly getting what I really wanted was beyond frustrating. Outwardly I was defiant and proud. Inwardly I was completely incensed and resentful. If it weren't for her unbelievably selfish addiction, maybe we could find financial aid dad could afford! The anger was simmering inside, boiling over at some point was unavoidable.

Chapter 10

January 7, 1994 started like most winter days around Western Washington, as I walked out to my car to leave for school it was cool outside, yet not bitterly cold. People from that area would consider a sweater sufficient for a morning in the low 40's with no wind or precipitation. Getting ready for school was just like any other day, dad had already left for work and mom was still sleeping off her alcohol.

First period was AP English with Mr. Cleeves, I loved that class. Even back then, I loved to read, interpret and debate literature then write about it. In class on that particular morning, we were talking Edgar Allan Poe, The Raven as memory serves. I was engaged in the class discussion, for being the shy introvert, there was something about Mr. Cleeves that drew me out. His passion and excitement over literature was genuine, and I appreciated that. Overhead, the PA crackled with a voice from the admin office:

"Sorry to interrupt Mr. Cleeves, please send Matt Whittington to the office."

Mr Cleeves nodded his head, said ok, smiled at me and motioned his hand toward the door. A few of the more immature kids in class did the whole cliché 'Oh you must be in troooouuuble' routine that kids do. I flushed a little, part embarrassment and part anger. I knew I'd done nothing wrong, more than anything I was just disoriented. *What could the office possibly want with me?*

As I slowly walked through the halls from class to the office I tried to make sense of this summons. Upon arriving at the office I didn't even have to sit and wait for a call back, the secretary sent me directly to the Vice Principal's office. My level of concern went up even more. *What's so serious that they rush me straight to the Vice Principal?*

The Vice Principal didn't say a word, he just handed me the phone. I said, hello, yet it was really in the form of a question. Through the phone I could hear a weepy voice, it was my mother's voice. She was able to compose herself long enough to say, "Matthew, your Papa died this morning, come home ok. Ok?" Then she hung up without a response from me.

Jack Edward King, the only grandfather I had ever known was gone. I had never known death for anyone close to me before, this was a completely new frontier. How could he be gone, it felt like I had just seen him days before, completely healthy. The fact was, he had been far from completely healthy though. A lifetime of excessive daily drinking had exacted a toll, a toll that all must pay among practicing alcoholics who refuse to quit drinking and get help. A death that while tragic and premature, was as certain as the day was long for a man too stubborn to listen to his doctor. The warning signs were there, Jack, my Papa was too stubborn to heed them. Of course I was not privy to the doctor's visits and recommendations Papa had made and received, but my Nana was. All of this information had been shared with my mom in the weeks following his death. So, there is no doubt in my mind that she was well aware that alcohol had ultimately killed her father. How seriously she would consider this warning? I never knew the extent of her concern. What was apparent, her drinking never slowed down.

***

Funeral services for Jack Edward King were held a few days later. The church service itself was very old school Catholic. Exceedingly long in duration were the services and without much character. I remember very little about the church service, just solemn words and prayers followed by a few tearful eulogies. Frankly most of the memories are indistinguishable until the point of graveside services. The procession eventually arrived at Evergreen Funeral Home in Everett, Washington. The same priest who had performed the service back at the church gave graveside services. I expected the customary military three volleys, the sailors firing their guns did not alarm me. What followed was absolutely stunning, Taps.

The lonely beautiful notes of Taps on a lone trumpet were gripping. I was caught off guard at first by the sailor in full white uniform standing alone in solitude from the hill above Papa's resting place. Then I couldn't take my eyes off him. Looking back it's quite unbelievable, yet true, I had never heard Taps. Unfolding in front of my eyes was something quite remarkable. As the sailor played the notes of Taps, it was as if the trumpet was crying. The trumpet was definitely crying and reaching out through the generations of sailors to say farewell to one of the United States Navy's finest. Twenty-four beautifully melancholy notes later the trumpet went silent. Everything was silent. In that sliver of time everything was sad, yet beautiful. I felt no anger. I felt no resentment. I felt no regrets. I felt no bitterness. The only feeling I had was a surreal pride as a folded flag was handed to Nana. I'm not saying Papa spoke to me, but the feelings and thoughts I had were; *alright Papa, I'll take it from here.*

Chapter 11

Following funeral services for Papa, I was more motivated than ever to prove I could still achieve my goal to be a fighter pilot. Up first on my to do list was get the recruiter on the phone. After a few attempts to call him, Sergeant Parker answered his phone. I asked him where we were at in the ROTC application process. The Sergeant said, "Oh yeah I was just going to call you. I got you an interview coming up. At the interview you'll have to do a fitness test, so bring a change of clothes." Man, I was stoked! The interview and fitness test were about a month off. I doubled down on the weights at school and worked harder on the dips, pushups, sit ups and pull ups. I drove a route around the neighborhood the high school was in until I had about three miles on the odometer and started running it every other day. I signed up to be an assistant coach for my little brother's little league team. On top of all that I still found time to squeeze in some hours at my part time job. I had taken my mind to the next level in terms of determination. The number of tasks I was allowing my mind to manage was far above my usual threshold.

One thing I had no room for was the escalation of my mom's addiction and the negative energy coming from her grief. I simply had no tolerance for drunk babbling, and I certainly felt anger over her dealing with things by drinking even more. Drowning herself in cheap beer wasn't going to bring back her dad, I found the behavior reprehensible and illogical. Where a normal kid in a family with no addict may rally to a parent with compassion and empathy, I responded with apathy and isolation. My mind was in a place of the future, while she had clearly gone somewhere much darker.

Leading up to that interview with the ROTC people my confidence was at an all-time high. For starters I was in great shape. I had never been a great runner, due in no small part to my unusually short legs, yet I had gotten my miles down to under 6:45. I was never particularly big as a teenager, at the time of my test I weighed under 135 pounds. Thanks to weight training I was able to bench press my body weight. I could do large amounts of dips and sit-ups, the only exercise that gave me problems was pull-ups. My dad had installed a pull-up bar in our backyard. I practiced at dead hang pull-ups and one-armed pull-ups. Still, the best I could manage was 15 pull-ups. So, that aspect of the fitness test did give me some concern, though I figured with my academic resume and good scores on everything else that I would be fine. I fully expected to earn that ROTC scholarship.

On the eve of my interview, I hardly slept. I was very nervous obviously, everything I had worked for hung in the balance of how the interview and physical fitness test went. After a few hours of restless sleep I drove to my recruiter's office in the morning. Upon arriving there, Sergeant Parker and I loaded up into his Ford Taurus and drove to North Seattle, Green Lake. The Sergeant pulled up to Green Lake and told me that we'd start with the three-mile run. Typically, I had been in the habit of finishing with the three-mile run after all the standard pull-ups and sit-ups. I wasn't particularly thrilled with the change in routine, but there was not much to be done about it. He gave me a few minutes to get stretched out and then off I went around the lake.

My nostrils flared to allow the brisk spring air into my lungs. It wasn't a cold morning by Seattle standards, perhaps low 50's. For the first mile I ran at about a 6:30 pace, just a little quicker than I trained. I dodged other runners, women with carriages and bicycles during my little dash. During the second mile, fatigue reared its ugly head and I slowed down. My short little legs felt heavy and numb, and I pushed through. Into the third mile I saw Sergeant Parker off in the distance. Motivation overcame me and I ran as fast as I could to the stopwatch. My lungs burned as they tried to suck in more of the cool lake air, and as I crossed the finish line I heard the number, 20:30. Perfect score for maximum points would have been 18:00 minutes, I had never run below 20:00, so the time was what I expected before starting. Still, I was a little disappointed after selling out over the last several hundred yards. During that mad dash I dreamed that maybe, just maybe I could pull out a phenomenal time.

After catching my breath the Sergeant and I loaded up in that gray government vehicle once more and made our way to the interview location. There he had me do the sit-ups, which I maxed out, and then pull-ups. I had very little recovery time between the run and sit-ups, and almost no recovery time between sit-ups and my weakest component, pull-ups. No excuses, I got up on that bar and from a dead hang position did 12 pull-ups. The Marines want to see 20. As I dropped off the bar the look of disappointment on Sergeant Parker's face was crushing. He said, "Get up there again, and this time kip your legs." I didn't know what the hell a kip was, and besides that I had hit muscle fatigue. So I got back up on that bar and exerted everything I had for another 5 pull-ups. The sets weren't cumulative, unfortunately, so the recorded number would be 12.

Finally, the time for the interview arrived. I would have thought that sitting in front of an officer to answer questions about my academic resume and life should have been more nerve racking. Perhaps it was the fatigue from giving maximum effort on the fitness test or maybe I was just confident, the nerves never came. I remember being calm. I remember being composed. Cocky? Maybe a little, I just felt really good about the interview. It was time to show off.

As the officer questioned me about school, my grades and sports I felt like things were really going well. GPA was just under 4.0 so things were rock solid there. Senior year of baseball was starting soon. He asked about the classes I was currently taking. I felt silly trying to rationalize why I had forgone advanced calculus and foreign languages for accounting and weight training. My interviewer then shook his head a little and raised eyebrows as he scribbled notes. Had I really just seen that? The body language was nearly imperceptible, yet I had seen a hint of disapproval. The officer then asked me about other extracurricular activities and community service. Besides coaching my brother's little league team I was pretty light on the extras. When did I have time for that? Charities? What did that have to do with being an officer? Admittedly I became a little flustered. I finally told the officer that besides little league I wasn't involved in any school clubs or community charities. Shortly after that, Sergeant Parker and I left. Things hadn't gone exactly as I would have expected, yet I felt pretty good about my chances.

Sergeant Parker didn't say much on the drive back.

***

Weeks later the phone rang at the house, I was outside mowing the yard. My mom stepped out to holler over the noise of my mower that I had a phone call. I jogged over to the phone expecting to hear the voice of a friend or work, it was Sergeant Parker.

I had been rejected for ROTC.

My heart sank. Deep down I knew the possibility existed, yet I had gotten my confidence and hope up so high, the news stung. I did my best to sound like a man as I asked him why. Sergeant Parker said, "You didn't do enough pull-ups, enough extracurricular and not enough community service." As Sergeant Parker continued talking, my mind went to disbelief.

Four-year academic letter, National Honor society and top ten in my class. Never mind that among the colleges sending me letters was Dartmouth and this guy is saying I'm not good enough because of pull-ups and extracurricular activities?!

I knew the recruiter had prepared me for this possibility, but how many of his recruits had my academic resume? If they're not going to find me good enough while all of my accomplishments were fresh, what difference would be made in my favor to be newly enlisted? If anything I only saw my stock trending down.

How could this happen? What the hell did school clubs or community service have to do with being a good officer and a good pilot? Did he really just say my pull-up numbers were a reason?! What, like I can't get to 20 pull-ups between that moment and officer training? As the recruiter rambled on more about upcoming pool functions and other nonsense I became angry. Did that dude really think that I cared about playing touch football at a pool function after he had just delivered news that had crushed my hopes? In that moment I didn't see future possibilities. I didn't think about working harder and trying again. I only processed one thought, it's over. Eighteen and my dreams were dead.

I didn't show up for the pool function Sergeant Parker had asked me about, nor did I show up for any others between that day and high school graduation. Sergeant Parker hadn't done anything wrong, but he had been the messenger that delivered bad news. I could not control where I was going after graduation, the contract ink had been dry for months. I could not control that the Marine Corps did not think I was officer material. What I could control was coordinating with my boss at the part time job to make sure he had me on the schedule for all pool function events. 'Sorry Sergeant Recruiter, I've got to work. I realize it's been months since you've seen me at a function. What do you want me to say? I don't control the schedule. You wouldn't encourage me to quit would you?'

Speaking of out of my control, there was my mom. How long is long enough when you believe someone to be grieving and drowning in their grief before you say something? The whole family lost the same person right? Sure, it was her father, but he was my grandfather. Could she not find time in her busy life of drinking like a fish to find sobriety long enough to check in on my mental and emotional health? Did she even care that I had worked my ass off for the past 7 years in school just to be told I'm not good enough for ROTC and shipped off to Marine Basic Training? She wasn't the only person with wrecked self-esteem, wrecked confidence, no social life and a heart full of dead dreams.

Whatever the reasons, I was sick of the denials and sick of the excuses. Drinking her life away and barely functioning as a parent was a lazy and selfish choice in my mind. One particular night dad had come home from work to the usual environment he must have become used to. I don't know what triggered the fight, but it was big. Real big. There was a lot of yelling, name calling and possibly a little contact. Not blows mind you. As I recall mom was obnoxiously in dad's face, it was a brutal verbal barrage on her part toward him. Dad managed to get away from her by moving her out of his way. Mom overreacted outrageously as if she were being outright abused. Dad got in his car and left. My little brother and sister were scared and not quite sure about what was going on. I was furious. From what I had seen, mom had picked this fight, no, ambushed dad when he got home. I'd had enough of her ridiculous emotional abuse towards my dad.

Boiling point, reached.

I got in her face.

Inches from her I went full volume. "Do you know why I'm leaving for the Marines?!"

The look on her face was stunned. She looked confused. She stank of nasty horse piss beer and her breath was hot on my face. Yet she said nothing.

"You, because of you! I hate you! I'm sick of you being too drunk to be a mom every day of my life! I can't take any more of this constant fighting! You are selfish! So sometime in the next few months maybe you'll wake up and miss me, I'll be gone from this hell and you'll wonder why. You, you are the reason why!"

You would think that a son telling a mom that he hates her would cut deep. It didn't. In fact from the look on her drunk face, it didn't even touch her in a remorseful way. Rather, she stepped closer to my face and opened her mouth to speak. I put a hand on each of her shoulders and pushed her away. I did not intend it to be hard. Maybe I was adrenalized or perhaps mom was at that point where the drunk was affecting her ability to stand. The reasons in retrospect do not matter. She fell over. Her fall seemed exaggerated to me, as if she were a flopping soccer player. Regardless the fact remains, I put hands on her and she tumbled. In that flash of a moment it felt good, and that feeling for that brief sliver of time has hung in remorse on my heart my whole life.

Eighteen years of living with an alcoholic had hurt my emotional and mental development more than I can quantify. I have no experience in what boys who don't have alcoholics for moms must feel. Do they get taught advanced guidance in communication skills with the opposite sex and coached through rejection? Do they get nurtured and coached on chasing their dreams? Are they in tune with a young boy's self-esteem and inadequacy issues enough to build them back up and empower them? Do they take personal pride in their son's accomplishments? Are they aware of what is troubling their kids, picking them up when they fall short and keeping their confidences? Are they a son's safe place?

My mom was none of those things. I felt cheated and robbed of a normal childhood. One of protection and nurturing. The Marine Corps was rising fast on my horizon and there were no do-overs in childhood. I missed out on so much because my mom was an alcoholic.

I knew she could have been much more, and for that I resented her.

Chapter 12

Familiar sights fade past as if my eyes are straining to register still shots of my childhood from the passenger seat of a government issued gray Ford Taurus. Bryant Field, where I played little league for the first time with my buddy Chad Arnold, sat empty and in desperate need of maintenance off to my right. I still remembered the first times I had donned the catcher gear, how big it was, and how proud I was to wear #8 in honor of Gary Carter. I remembered the blue jerseys, I remembered the white trim and most of all I remembered how bad we were at baseball. God how I loved it. That was when I was still a child, a lifetime ago.

Above the shin high grass and weed filled infield stood the old backstop. Even now I recall how it seemed stooped as if in reflection of my melancholy. Above the backstop and trees, gray clouds have gathered to block out the sun, just as clouds have covered my mind and soul.

A voice penetrates the malaise, "Your family loves you very much, I will keep in touch with them to let them know how you're doing." As if you'll know dumbass. Where are you going to be? Instead I just mumble back to the voice and nodded my head.

My eyes search for other familiar images to cling to. We pass the turn for Kackman Road where some of my closest friends lived and then descended on the final stretch of Highway 9 before entering Arlington proper. The car navigates over a bridge spanning the Stillaguamish River, images of the girl who lost her life in that river float through my mind, Andrea Short. She left Arlington too.

That voice interrupts me again.

"Get down there, work hard and stand out. Be a badass. Try to graduate as squad leader."

While I nodded in acknowledgement, on the inside I laughed. This advice stood in stark contrast to the advice my dad had proffered maybe an hour prior.

Dad had said, "Son, I'm proud of all that you have accomplished. You have nothing to prove to me. Keep your head down, follow orders and don't make waves. Drill Instructors pick on the ones that make waves. You'll be ok." Words of wisdom from the mouth of the man who survived some of the most violent combat in 1970 Vietnam. I made mental note; *benefit of the doubt to dad over Sergeant Parker on this.*

A few minutes later the Taurus was at freeway speed, pointed South on Interstate 5 toward Seattle. Like a ship that fades from view before disappearing into the fog, Arlington faded into my past. In my heart I knew there would be visits and reunions with family and friends, but the mousy shy boy from Bryant was gone. Forever. Final glances at my parents when I got into that car had told me as much. The story told by the looks I got from my younger sister and brother told a different tale, betrayal. I was running away. Legally, yet still running away. While there would be no such salvation for them. Big brother would not be around anymore to shield or deflect the ugly monster of alcoholism.

41st Street in Everett passed by and my eyes snapped to the right to look for an image I wanted burned into my retinas before leaving for good. There, on the hill overlooking the Interstate, Evergreen Funeral Home. Papa's final resting place.

As the lush green grass of the cemetery disappears from view, I closed my eyes. I wanted to remember the entirety of Papa's graveside service just six months past. Only the eloquent beauty of Taps returns to my brain with clarity. Perfect white uniform. That sailor was unassuming, yet reverent. Where one might have expected rigid perfection and clinical execution of duties; I saw an emotional connection to a man the sailor could not have possibly known personally. Something intangible connected the men who wore the same uniform 50 years apart.

Perhaps Sergeant Parker sensed my need to process what was happening, or maybe the guy had run out of clichés and hyperbole. Either way, he finally got to a point where no more words were coming out of his mouth and I was grateful for the quiet. Congratulations dude, one more sucker was on his way to Basic Training. I was one more warm body closer to his quota.

With all that was familiar far behind, my mind shifted to the road ahead. The future.

The date was June 25, 1994. I was on my way to some low budget hotel somewhere between SeaTac Airport and Seattle MEPS. Once checked in, I was expected to be well rested for an early wakeup call and long day of processing at Seattle MEPS. As hotel rooms go, the place I was stashed at was nothing special, even for an 18-year-old. I found the one luxury that a kid who grew up on two antenna channels could find, Sportscenter.

So there I sat, in a cheap hotel chair watching Sportscenter, with nothing to do but reflect over this crossroads moment in my life. Roads behind. The decisions I had made and what consequences they portended for the future. Roads ahead. Damn, did I really even *want* to be a Marine? I wanted to be a Marine fighter pilot, flying F-18s or Harriers, not some grunt. Sure I would have to do this Basic Training at some point, but why the rush?

Alcoholism, that was why the rush. I was sick of the hatred and resentment; those things were poisoning me from the inside out. The worst part was, I felt an utter lack of control over those emotions. I didn't want to be hateful. I didn't want to be angry or resentful. What I did want was for the turmoil and tumult to stop. I wanted peace in my life. I wanted to live somewhere where I didn't have to hear my parents screaming at each other. I didn't care where that was, just so long as the drinking and screaming stopped.

I began to wonder what other people were doing right then as I sat all alone and isolated from the world. Did my family miss me? Were my parents crying? I was fairly certain my mom would use this event as yet another excuse to drink herself into oblivion. As if she needed an excuse. And then, I began to hate her on a whole new level. 'No. No you don't get to use MY decisions or the ensuing consequences as an excuse to further that despicable habit mom. NO. This is mine and you have no right to it. This may suck, but at least it won't suck with you as part of it. Drink all you want, not my problem anymore. Just don't drink over me, you don't have my permission.'

And then, I cried.

I ugly cried.

Why the hell did I cry?

***

Shortly after my silly blubbering subsided, the assigned 'roommate' entered the room. Now that was a surprise. Here I thought I had scored a room all to myself, issues and all, for the night. The United States Military saw it differently. Not only did I have the pleasure of a roommate, I had the pleasure of a drunk roommate with a case of beer under his arm and two guests in tow, both were girls. Even on this first night, sans drunk mom, I would have to endure yet another obnoxious drunk. From what I could tell as he stood there looking ridiculous with the door open, he was not the only one. I noticed what I had been oblivious to before, a whole hallway full of crazy drunks. The irony was not lost on me. There was no escape.

Wakeup call the following morning came way too fast. That hotel was an out of control party zone all night, what sleep I did manage was brief and restless. The shuttle bus to MEPS stunk of beer, sweat and shame. Thankfully the ride was short. For as brief as the trip to MEPS was, the rest of the day would feel like the longest day ever.

Most of what I recall about going through the MEPS process is all the medical exams. A team of doctors, nurses and interns were there to poke and prod and examine everything about your body. I think they were looking for reasons to reject me. Hearing tests. Vision tests. Cardiovascular, respiratory, and on and on it went. I began to get nervous, did they expect something to be wrong with me? Did they see something I was unaware of? Before long I realized the reality of being in the military, they didn't know who I was. I was just another in a long line of faceless recruits to them. Just another cog on the assembly line that is the enlistment process of our United States Military. Once I gained situational awareness, the monotony became easier. Go there, see that doc. Next go there, wait 30 minutes for that doc. And so on and so on. Finally, there comes a point where all the boxes are checked and this team of medical staff are content with your health and hence fit for duty. That is when a group of recruits gets ushered to a small room with a flag in it and an officer issues an oath:

'I, Matthew Henry Whittington, do solemnly swear that I will support and defend the Constitution of the United States against all enemies, foreign and domestic; that I will bear true faith and allegiance to the same; and that I will obey the orders of the President of the United States and the orders of the officers appointed over me, according to regulations and the Uniform Code of Military Justice. So help me God.'

The date was June 26, 1994.

With the oath taken we're off to SeaTac Airport. I had been booked on a flight to Marine Corps Recruit Depot in San Diego, California aboard Delta with a stop in Reno, Nevada. The plane departed around dusk and I had a window seat. Views of the sunset over Washington; Mount Rainier and Mount St. Helens were stunning. As the plane gained in altitude, the only home I had ever known fell away, far below. Ironic, the only thing I had dreamed about doing in our military was essentially the first stage in this journey I was on, flying. This. This feeling of freedom above the clouds is all I ever wanted with my life. All my dreams were there, all of my cares and worldly problems were far below. How on Earth did I let that recruiter talk me into something less than my dream? I wanted that flight to last forever. I didn't want that plane to ever land.

I knew I needed sleep. Sleep would be such a precious commodity in the very near future, but I couldn't. I thought a lot about my dad. What was my dad doing right now? Was he worried? Did he miss me? Was he crying? I thought about my little sister, Sarah. She would turn 13 while I was becoming a Marine. How was she handling being the oldest? I thought about my little brother, John. He was only 10. No big brother around anymore to equal parts torture and protect him. How would he handle life without me around? It's not like I hung out with him, would John even notice the difference in my absence? I thought about my neighbor and buddy, Chad Arnold. Who was he going to play catch with? Damn, I knew I needed sleep, my brain just wouldn't shut down.

That layover in Reno didn't last very long. I seriously thought, *'What would happen if I just walked out of this airport and lived the life of a drifter?'* If I got on that next plane they had me. I envisioned a Drill Instructor waiting for me at the end of the jet way to take me away. Where else could I go? Who else did I know?

Nowhere, nobody.

I took an oath. *I* made a commitment. *I* signed that contract. Nobody in my family had ever earned the title, United States

Marine. *Nobody.* I *would* be the first. I *wanted* to be the first.

I got on that plane.

As the Boeing 737 climbed into the darkness I looked out the window. I saw nothing. Just darkness. There was nothing to admire and distract my mind. Fear overwhelmed me, I cried softly into the window. Then I thought about my Papa. What did he feel when that Kamikaze dove into the ship he was on out in the Pacific 50 years ago? Did he cry? What did my dad feel when they loaded him on a plane destined for Vietnam? Did he cry? What the hell was wrong with me? Those things dad and Papa did, those things were real dangers. They had real problems. Why was I worried about men yelling at me and making me exercise? Surely if they could survive war, I could survive 13 weeks of Marine Basic Training. Right?

Then, I slept.

Chapter 13

I'm not a big fan of buses, but I wanted that bus from San Diego Airport to Marine Corps Recruit Depot to go as slow as possible. The driver did not accommodate my wishes of course, that ride was ridiculously short.

Yellow footprints. Rows upon rows of yellow footprints, all in perfect alignment with heels touching in such a way that the space between feet creates a 45-degree angle. I thought, 'How nice, they know exactly where we need to stand and how to put our feet, this is going to be easy.' Oh my God was I ever wrong.

How can so many people screw up standing?! Seriously?

My fellow bus riders and I must have been the largest gaggle of completely inept morons to ever try standing as I heard this Drill Instructor tell it. Luckily I managed to attract very little attention with only slight corrections made to my posture as the Drill Instructor walked by. I heard other guys get screamed at for such things as speaking and asking to use the bathroom.

The Drill Instructor was finally able to get everyone standing how he wanted them. At that time we were shuffled off to a phone bank and given strict instructions about how the phone call home would go. We were told there would be no tolerance for conversation, the call was simply to inform your parents or spouses that you had safely arrived at the Marine Recruit Depot and that they should expect written correspondence. I dialed home and Dad answered the phone. The conversation was painfully short.

"Hey Dad, I'm safe here at boot camp you'll be getting letters from me soon." Dad told me he loved me and asked if I was alright. In strict compliance with the Drill Instructor's directions I said, "Yes, gotta go." Then I hung up.

Following the gut-wrenching phone call the rest of the night was a blur. We got the iconic first boot camp haircuts and uniform issue. The hour was very late before we were led to a dorm to get some sleep.

***

Reveille came very fast; the sleep was really more of a glorified power nap than actual REM sleep. Breakfast was much needed and very brief. The Drill Instructor was in a big hurry to get us places. There was a lot of processing that required my name, signature and social security number. Following hours of signing papers, the platoon of recruits was led to get immunizations. We were made to sit on the floor "A to B" which is to say Asshole to Balls. A recruit that day was in constant contact with other recruits. The entire in processing experience was a zombified sleep deprived blur.

I think processing took maybe a few days, not long at all. I remember thinking the Drill Instructor leading us around was not as bad as I was warned. I thought maybe I had struck a lucky break; Marine Boot Camp was not going to break me down after all. I was so very wrong.

Once processing was done the platoon was led to a squad bay and arranged in a semi-circle near the front door. The Drill Instructor informed us that the time had come for the platoon to be handed over for training.

Next, four Drill Instructors lined up in front of us. A scarier more intimidating sight I do not recall. The Platoon Commander gave a speech about how to report abuse and introduced the four Drill Instructors standing behind him. Our Senior Drill Instructor was Staff Sergeant Becerra. Rounding out the training team were Drill Instructor Sergeants Buck, Crane and Cullen. Our Platoon Commander said a few more words before giving way to our Senior. Staff Sergeant Becerra gave a brief synopsis about what he expected from his platoon of recruits and what we recruits should expect from the Drill Instructors. Once the introductions and expectations were complete, the Senior turned the Sergeants loose on us.

In the moment those three high energy Drill Instructors are released upon a platoon, I can tell you that no other cares, worries, issues or thoughts last long on the conscience. The only thing that matters in that moment is self-preservation. How could I minimize their focus on me? I didn't think about my dad, my mom, my siblings or friends. I didn't think about baseball, cars or girls. All I thought about was focusing on doing exactly what those Sergeants wanted as fast as possible. Those who have lived through similar experiences could tell you, there is simply no way to hide and get through without drawing the ire of a Drill Instructor. At some point you will make a mistake and somehow they never miss mistakes.

My first slip came in the first ten minutes of the Senior cutting his team loose. For starters, Drill Instructors are damn funny. The skill of zeroing in on a man's flaws or insecurities so quickly and picking at the nerves to the point of breaking is a special skill, and Sergeant Buck had it. Sergeant Buck had picked out a recruit who couldn't figure out how to talk properly, the recruit was stuttering and stumbling through his sirs and Sergeant Buck was all over him, I thought the kid might cry. In retrospect, that may be part of the point. Who can function at a high level under pressure? Who's going to break at the first signs of adversity? Of course I thought I had their system all figured out, I could simply watch the blunders of other recruits and learn from them. I could discreetly exploit the misfortunes of the other guys to make myself blend in and seem unremarkable. I was very wrong.

I made the very dire mistake of turning my head, ever so slightly and grinning just a little. After all, it was funny, mostly because it wasn't me. Then, it happened. Sergeant Buck's peripheral detection of movement was incredible. From 20 feet away he saw the slight movement of my neck and grin. Before I knew it, the Sergeant was inches from my face correcting everything about me. My posture. The alignment of my thumbs with the seams of my trousers. The angle created in the negative space between my feet in regard to my heels and toes. My bearing. I had no idea that I didn't know how to stand properly. He even insulted the gap in my teeth.

Day one of life in Alpha Company Platoon 1030, 90 recruits.

Shortly after the shock and awe campaign by the three Drill Instructors on the recruits of 1030, we were ordered outside to form up. The first formation we were re-arranged by height from tallest to shortest so I wound up about ¾ of the way back and in 3rd squad. We were drilled on facing movements and how to pivot to where you are ensured to end up with the desired 45-degree angle. It didn't take long before the entire platoon was messing up on a regular basis and the Drill Instructors decided to take us to the sand pit for the first time. The sand pit is where the platoon goes to get their asses kicked. Intense PT (Physical Training) to the point of muscle fatigue is the point of this dreaded punishment. Side straddle hops (jumping jacks), pushups, sit ups, flutter kicks, and running in place (HIGH KNEES HIGH KNEES) are all done to a four count in repetitions. 1, 2, 3 …. ONE! 1, 2, 3 … TWO and so on until you struggle to do them at all. The Drill Instructors hover over and move around from recruit to recruit to make sure they are being done correctly and if they catch a recruit half assing the PT, the whole platoon is made aware and we keep going until they, the Drill Instructors, get sick of watching us. You hear them say things like, "There's no draft, you *volunteered* to be here recruit! I didn't *make* you sign those papers recruit, push!"

I didn't realize from the bus ride in and subsequent days of going to and from chow just how close San Diego Airport was to MCRD until we were mired in one of these sand pits. MCRD literally shares a fence with the airport and you can see the planes taking off right over your head. The thought that kept repeating in my head while doing endless flutter kicks, covered in sand, feet blistered and sweating my ass off was: *I wish I was on that plane right now.*

Frankly in the chaos of the first days of learning to march, physical training, classes and more marching you lose track of the days of the week and just count time by chow. Breakfast, lunch and dinner account for about 30 minutes a day where you have relative peace while speed eating. After dinner you look forward to lights out and about 4-6 hours of sleep and peace from the Drill Instructors before you wake up the next morning and hit it hard again. I especially remember while standing out on that hot parade deck noting all the Southwest Airlines planes jetting out of town, it was torture. During one of our drill sessions, Drill Instructor Sergeant Buck was attempting to teach us left and right oblique. Recruits kept pivoting on wrong feet and turning the wrong way, we couldn't get anything right. Platoon 1030 was a total cluster fuck. He finally got fed up with our total ineptitude and off to the pits we went. All three of our Drill Instructors were firm and tough, though Sergeant Buck seemed to truly enjoy thrashing us in the pits the most. He bore a striking resemblance to the liquid Terminator from Terminator 2, and I feared him more that's for sure. I believe we were doing pushups and Sergeant Buck was pushing us to and past the point of fatigue. One recruit got up and made a run for the fence separating MCRD from San Diego airport. He was tackled by a Drill Instructor before making the fence, I never saw that guy again. When I laid my head down that night I thought, *there is no escape.*

The next day platoon 1030 was taken out by the obstacle course to work out with logs by Sergeant Crane. Log work out is a difficult work out due to the weight of the logs and the disparity in work load among squad members, some guys seem to conserve their energy and let other recruits work harder. I'm not saying guys outright cheated, but I know when a guy isn't giving his all when there is a gap between his shoulder and the log. At any rate we survive the work out and then it's on to the obstacle course.

You may have some idea what the obstacle course is like if you've seen Full Metal Jacket. The "Stairway to Heaven" is the tall ladder you climb then throw your leg over and climb down. It's very tall. There is also rappelling which was actually very fun. There are things you climb over, jump over and ropes you hang from and move hand over hand until the obstacle is traversed. After all of that, Sergeant Crane took us to the rope climb. I struggled with the rope climb already because I had not yet learned the importance of putting the workload on your legs. I was essentially trying to climb the thing using only upper body strength. On this day and after all that exertion with the logs and obstacle course, I was spent. Most recruits made it all the way up, I on the other hand made it about 2/3 of the way up and hit full muscle fatigue and couldn't get any higher. Sergeant Crane was screaming at me, "Get up that rope recruit!" I was not able to muster any more strength and I slid down the rope to a blistering Sergeant Crane. On our way to chow the Drill Instructor stopped us at the pull up bars, I did maybe 8 dead hang pull ups. Sergeant Crane was incensed.

After chow the platoon was taken out to do more drill, we screwed it all up again and back to the pit the platoon went. Remedial PT until we were soaked in sweat and the Drill Instructor got sick of our grunting in the sand. I distinctly recall just wanting to quit on that day. I wanted to tell them, "Look I made a mistake send me home" but knew that they would just tell me I'd signed a contract. I survived the day and the Drill Instructor finally gave my favorite order, "Sleep recruits." All I could think about laying in my bunk was how bad I wanted to be on one of those planes. I felt lied to by my recruiter. I felt alone. I couldn't envision a way through or the reward of graduation day. I wanted to cry. My muscles ached and there were blisters on my feet and I knew it was only going to be a few short hours until reveille and we'd do it all again.

The sun went down and I caught glimpse of a flash out the squad bay window. I turned my head and looked, it was fireworks. The day was July 4, 1994 and I was watching fireworks over San Diego. My favorite holiday as a kid was Independence Day. My dad would buy tons of fireworks from the reservation and we'd spend all day lighting off firecracker cans, bottle rockets and the like before finishing the night with those balls that went into mortar tubes for the colorful stuff. Independence Day and I am anything but independent. I cried. The timing of what would happen next was so profound that it still grips my emotions to this day, Taps. Taps played right then under the fireworks. My mind washed over what those notes meant and the sacrifices that had been made long before me. The fight for life my dad suffered in the worst years of Vietnam. My Papa's fight for life as the Ommaney Bay sunk and his fellow sailors died there in the Sulu Sea while he swam to rescue. Most importantly I remembered Taps from Papa's service seven months prior. I stared out the window and thought about all the men and women who had served before me during conflicts; I thought about all of the men and women who would follow in conflict in years to come. Surely I could survive 12 more weeks of Marine Recruit training. It was in those moments my resolve solidified and my determination to succeed and not be broken grew. It was that night, alone in my bunk under fireworks and Taps that I said to myself; in moments of weakness I will internalize Taps. I will not let my Papa, my dad, or myself down. I will be a United States Marine.

Chapter 14

To say the remainder of Marine Recruit training was easy would be both dishonest and insulting. What had changed in my mind overnight was a paradigm shift of mental attitude not a physical transformation. I did learn by watching recruits who the Drill Instructors called their "rabbits" how to use the "kip" on pull ups and push with my legs on the rope. The "kip" was widely used at the time; it's a way of synchronizing your legs in a kick and rocking your body while doing pull ups, essentially harnessing momentum to conserve upper body strength. The practice of using the "kip" would be banned in my later years of service. Within weeks and before phase two of Basic Training, I was making it up the rope easily every time and went from 10-12 dead hang pull ups to a peak of 31. Platoon 1030 soon coalesced into a passable drilling platoon.

Drill was still a lot of work and PT was of course PT, they were challenging. I no longer dreaded them as soul crushing events where I felt the Drill Instructors were trying to break us; rather I viewed them as a challenge to set new highs and attain perfection. We started to hear praise from our Drill Instructors and when I finally heard positivity and pride from Sergeant Buck my motivation soared. Phase 1 was coming to an end and platoon 1030 was being taken to Camp Pendleton for phase 2, weapons and field training.

Camp Pendleton California, home to the 1st Marine Division, Marine Combat Training and for the next few weeks platoon 1030. Here they trained us on the M-16A2 service rifle. The instructors training recruits on the rifle range are far more laid back than a standard Drill Instructor, I assume it is because the weapons are loaded for real and nobody wants a guy losing his mind out there. Those range instructors have to be among the finest in the world. We trained at 200, 300 and 500 yards with iron sights. Hitting the target at 200 and 300 yards after some practice was easy enough, hitting from 500 with iron sights was significantly more challenging.

Other skills taught in phase 2 are setting up encampments with tents, learning to pack all your equipment into a ruck, learning about different patrol formations, biological warfare, gas chamber and field sanitation. Additionally, we did a lot of "humps" which are essentially long hikes with full gear, equipment on your back and rifles. During that portion of phase 2 is when the Senior Drill Instructor really seemed to be around the platoon a lot more. Instead of the regular cadence from the Sergeants, Staff Sergeant Becerra would do what sounded like a sing song type cadence. It was different to feel that kind of motivation and attention from the Senior, it felt like we were turning the corner as a platoon and I found it very motivating. During one of these humps I tweaked a knee and spent a few days on light duty. They threatened to drop me to another platoon if I was not able to get back. My knee was not fully recovered, but I forced myself back in and gritted out the remainder of training. Platoon 1030 started together, I wanted to finish together.

When phase 2 wrapped up the platoon traveled back to MCRD. By this point the finish line is in sight and you start getting salty, a little cocky even. Back at MCRD the Senior Drill Instructor took us out for drill to get the platoon accustomed to his voice and cadence for final review. Senior was the one who would be out there for final inspections and graduation. One particular day the platoon may have been a little too cocky or maybe a little out of focus. The Senior was enraged and what followed was one of the worst thrashings of all Basic Training. The man I thought to be like my dad within the Corps thrashed us in a pit until the entire platoon was at full exhaustion, and then he thrashed us a little more. I was never so happy to see Sergeant Buck who followed up the Senior that day.

The last weeks of training Sergeant Buck was still firm and tough, but he'd shifted from recruit killer to the man the platoon seemed to respect and motivate for the best. We were a little louder for Sergeant Buck, and I think at least, we did everything he asked of us with a little more edge. He sensed it too. Sergeant Buck didn't outright smile, but you could detect when his lips would ever so slightly turn upwards, a grin perhaps.

In the waning weeks of Basic Training the platoon did swim qualifications, final drill and final PFT (Physical Fitness Test.) My final PFT numbers were 27 pull ups, 90 sit ups in two minutes and a 20-minute three-mile run.

Through letters from my parents I learned the family was taking a train down for graduation. We had a day in training to make arrangements for leave after Basic so I requested two weeks and bought a train ticket back with my parents. The company rehearsed graduation for days until we had it mastered. With graduation a few days away I got my uniforms for after Basic squared away and as promised in my contract the PFC (Private First Class E2) stripe was sewn onto my uniforms. Additionally, Sergeant Buck read off MOS assignments. "Recruit Whittington, 6154, Airframes. You mean to tell me you're air wing?!" I didn't dare laugh even though it reminded me of Full Metal Jacket when the Drill Instructor reads off Joker's assignment to journalism.

The day before graduation I was able to visit my family, it was wonderful to see them. My parents smiled a lot and marveled at my physical transformation. Dad was smiling and mom was sober, it was incredible. I was on top of the world. My little brother and sister seemed happy to see me as well. I regaled them in the trials and tribulations of what I'd been through and my parents said over and over, "You are just standing taller." I was standing taller. What I had been through in the first weeks of Marine Recruit Training had changed me. For the first time in my life I felt as though I might fail at something and the pride I felt from resolving to not be broken and exceeding beyond my expectations made me very proud. In the morning I would be a United States Marine.

September 16, 1994, graduation day. Platoon 1030 formed up for ceremonies along with the rest of Alpha Company, albeit significantly smaller in numbers from where we started 13 weeks prior. Our platoon began with a robust number of 90 recruits, 53 graduated on time. With the company assembling I look for my family in the crowd and had no success spotting them.

Around 1000 the graduation gets under way. Senior Drill Instructor Staff Sergeant Becerra stood in front of us as all the other Seniors stood in front of their respective platoons. We marched out on the parade deck in front of the bleachers, once finally in place I was able to spot my dad. The remainder of the ceremony remains a blur years later; there was some music, some speeches and finally it wrapped up and we were dismissed as United States Marines.

Chapter 15

After graduation, our family boarded the train in San Diego for a ride along the coast, going home. I would have preferred flying, but dad really wanted to see the coast from a train so we did. The trip took a few days, the scenery was nice and mom was still sober. Having a sober mom to talk to might have been my favorite part of the trip. It sounds so simple, but I could actually talk to my mom. She showed interest and engaged in conversation about Marine Basic Training and what would be next for me. When I told her about Taps and how I thought about Papa every day, she cried. I hugged her and it meant everything. I can't tell you a single other thing about that train ride, but those conversations with my mom meant a lot to me.

***

Pulling into that driveway where I stood every morning waiting for the bus as a kid felt like sliding on a broken in pair of tennis shoes. I may have been gone three months, yet the driveway looked no different. The house looked no different. Walking into the house however, felt completely different. My room wasn't my room anymore. My sister had acquired it. The house seemed a little cleaner, and I felt like a guest. The house wasn't my home anymore.

Turned out a funny thing happened in my three-month absence, life went on. My sister and brother seemed happy to have me around, yet they were different. They evolved. My sister in particular seemed stronger with more emotional callous. In three months she seemed to transform from little baby sister to independent teen. My little brother was still little brother, just a little more assertive. He asked me to come and visit his classroom to talk to them about life as a Marine, so I did. The class went on to write me periodically that school year, like a pen pal.

The first night back home, we had a backyard barbeque. Dad grilled up my favorite, boneless pork ribs as only he has ever done perfectly the way I like. There was also corn on the cob, fruit cocktail and baked beans. I drank Coca Cola. Mom drank beer, a lot of beer. I did not know what stress, real or perceived, could have possibly precipitated the need to be totally wasted that night, yet there she was. So drunk it looked like she was swaying to only music she could hear. The old undertow of anger rushed back. I do not know what made me think she could be sober for that one night so that our family could finally be whole and enjoy those fleeting moments of fellowship and togetherness. Maybe it was the amazing feeling I had from our train ride home that lulled me into a false sense of change and a new chapter. Perhaps I wanted to believe that having her oldest son out of reach for three months was enough to compel at least some effort at sobriety. Whatever the reason, I was a damn fool. My mom had no intention of living a sober life, whether I was there or not, and that fact lit an inferno of rage inside me.

I was ready to move on. Home was not home anymore. I did not have a home, just orders.

***

Marine Combat Training takes place at Camp Pendleton for West Coast Marines. After leave, I flew back into San Diego to report for MCT. I caught a shuttle up to Camp Pendleton from San Diego and reported for duty. They assigned me to Hotel Company, 4th platoon 4th squad and I was put into a Quonset hut for the night. I remember getting an upper bunk and thinking of the weird adjustment I still hadn't quite made from Recruit to Marine. The programming was still there, the urge to call NCOs "sir" was still there. The next morning a bunch of us were gathered into a building and given a briefing about MCT and how liberty works. I distinctly remember being told that no Marine is to purchase a car while there, which I thought was funny. We were warned about drinking on base and not venturing too far away from base in the days off we would have. Obviously, in retrospect these warnings were all made necessary by dumb ass Privates who did not know how to act.

Every Marine is a basically trained rifleman, and that's what MCT is all about. Every Marine is taught fire teams, weapon familiarization for different weapons, land navigation, how to dig fighting holes, chemical warfare preparedness and much more. In what order these skills were taught, I do not recall, I do however remember a great deal of the experience as a whole.

The first thing I recall is that the Sergeant in charge of our platoon treated us only slightly better than a recruit. It seemed to me at the time that his attitude was like 'This is a shitty assignment and I don't want to be here.' He didn't give off the motivational vibe I'd become accustomed to from the Drill Instructors, the Sergeant was more relaxed and matter of fact about training.

We marched or "humped" everywhere we went. The Sergeant taught us how to pack for humps, how to wear our gear and how to keep our feet from blistering too bad.

There were Marines who came back from liberty and it was obvious they had found ways to drink. As it turned out, the E-Club (E for Enlisted) would serve alcohol if you were under 21. Despite all the warnings in briefing about drinking, nothing happened to those who came back from doing so. I would imagine it was because they (the leadership) knew that Marines could do so legally on base, though the message I got was that it was more about covering their asses than actually enforcing the standards that had been set. This was my first lesson on the alcohol culture of the Marine Corps. What the leadership was saying in their silence was, 'we are going to advise you not to drink, but if you do just don't do anything stupid to put us in the funny papers.' In the beginning, it aggravated me how the Marine Corps enabled the alcoholic culture that I knew very well. My entire reason for using the Marine Corps to get away from alcoholism completely backfired. I simply traded one drunk for hundreds.

***

After combat training, I was sent to Naval Air Station Millington in Tennessee. NAS Millington is where the Navy and Marine Corps send people to get training for aircraft maintenance. The living accommodations were the best I would know to that point in military life, two men to a room. No squad bays or Quonset huts. I ended up with a good Marine from Pennsylvania. For many Marines and sailors at Millington, this duty assignment was their first time with no instructors dictating the nightly schedules. No humps or forced PT. Just classwork every day and liberty every night.

By and large most of the guys I knew went out clubbing and drinking every night. The most popular of which were places like The Pyramid and the Neon Moon. I went out a few times to see what those places were all about; truth is clubs were not really my scene. Even at 19, I just was not into partying. I preferred to study and learn my job. Mechanics did not then and still do not come naturally to me. So I mostly studied to learn hydraulic principles and how to differentiate and identify types of corrosion. While many Marines and sailors were drinking every night, I was studying. I had no desire to drink with them, the behavior sickened me. I had a reputation as a loner; maybe they thought I was weird. I did not care.

I called home a lot. I was lonely. I didn't know how to talk to those people, my fellow Marines. I didn't speak their language. Back then, nobody had cell phones or unlimited data. I had to spend money on calling cards, lots of money. Most of my pay went to calling home. I needed my dad. I needed someone who understood what it meant to be far away from family and friends and lonely as hell. We talked a lot, hours. We would talk about my day and what I was learning. We would talk about what aircraft I might work on and where that would take me. We would talk about his day. We would talk about Janet the drunk, and I would get angry for him. I would get angry at her refusal to choose sobriety for her husband and two remaining kids. We talked about everything, my dad was my best friend. I could not have persevered without his support and wisdom.

Near the end of training at NAS Millington the instructors read off the airframe assignments. I wanted fast movers, Hornets or Harriers. I did not get what I wanted. "Whittington, Hueys and Cobras. Camp Pendleton." I was disappointed.

That night I called my dad and told him where I had been assigned. Dad was so excited for me. He reminded me of the history of Hueys and Cobras, specifically how they started in Vietnam. He reminded me of all the Hueys he'd ridden on and of all the lives they saved getting soldiers out of hot zones, out of harm's way. He reminded me about the need for Cobras in Vietnam and how the birth of the airframe changed warfare. He reminded me how his life was undoubtedly saved along with the lives of his comrades thanks to Hueys and Cobras. He then asked if I remembered the one aircraft he had a Polaroid of in his modeling craft box, an AH-1 Cobra. Nobody made lemonade from lemons for me like my dad could. In one conversation he had turned me from melancholy to feeling like things were turning out how they were meant to be.

Chapter 16

I reported to HMLA-369 at Camp Pendleton early in 1995, the Gunfighters. Frankly I was a little scared of the unknown, there was no more schooling or training, it was time to get to work. Upon completing checking in with admin I was sent to the airframe shop where I would be working. A Gunnery Sergeant, or Gunny, as they are known in the Corps was the first person to greet me. The guy seemed very old. The Gunny gave some generic advice about learning and attitude before introducing me to the Sergeants. Past experience warned me that Sergeants are ruthless mean bastards so I was very quiet and respectful. The Sergeants who were present on my first day were rough alpha personalities, but they seemed to treat me well with relatively harmless hazing.

Once all the introductions were made, someone at the squadron took me over to the barracks to get settled in. I ended up getting a barracks room with another guy who had just arrived, he was from Ohio. That guy ended up being a severe drunk who partied all the time, he even came back from a weekend trip once with only one shoe. I just shook my head. I could not understand what in the minds of these other young men made them behave like this. Was it a relative lack of supervision that made them go crazy? Whatever the reason, it pissed me off. I had no more control over alcohol in my life than I did as a boy at home.

I called home to talk to my dad about the frustrations I was having with drunks everywhere I looked. I sat down at the pay phone to make the call and mom answered the phone, drunk. My body felt rigid. My face felt flushed. My knuckles were white from the fists I was making.

I said, "Hi, mom."

Mom's response was slurred, I could just envision her standing there swaying with glossed over eyes, "Hey Matthew, how you doing?"

I replied, "Fine mom. Is dad home? Can you put him on the phone please?"

And so it went. No matter what I did to get alcohol out of my life, it was everywhere. All encompassing. The culture of dealing with drunks was not just part of the DNA of my childhood, it was becoming the way of life in adulthood. There was no escape, nowhere in the world I could go to eliminate drunks from my life. I felt hopeless. Trapped. A six-year contract seems like a lifetime at 19 years old. I signed the contract. I signed up for, this?

I said to my dad when he got on the phone, "Dad, my roommate is a partying drunk. Changing roommates isn't likely to help, they are ALL drunks it seems like. They are everywhere. In my barracks room, outside my barracks room and in all the surrounding barracks rooms. There's no place for me to go. What do I do? I don't know if I can handle this, I don't know if I'm going to make it. I'm lonely. I can't even escape for a little while with no car. I just don't know what to do."

I cried.

Through the phone I felt my father's sense of helplessness, understanding and empathy. What could he say? What could I reasonably expect? What kind of impossible position was I putting my dad in, there was no way to save me. We both knew that.

My dad said, "Son, you just have to find a way to make the most of it. I know you're lonely and things seem bad right now. It will not always be this way. Find some hobbies, find some things to do outside of the barracks. Focus on learning your job. Have good enthusiasm at work so that you learn more. Find some people who share some common interests. I know you're lonely and we do miss you, but we're very proud of you. Keep your chin up, it's all going to work out ok."

I felt like such a child. My lip quivered and I fought so hard to not let him hear me cry. I wanted him to feel ok and not be worried yet let him feel as though he'd been inspiring and helpful.

I failed.

Tears were flowing and I was openly sobbing. I simply said, "Ok dad, I gotta go. Love you." He said he loved me back and I hung up.

What I did next was immature, it felt wrong, and I swore I would never do it. I didn't know what else to do. I didn't know how to survive for 6 years with these new brothers and sisters of mine if I couldn't fit in.

I drank with them.

***

As it turns out, a large group of drunks are only obnoxious when viewed through the prism of sobriety. Once a person consumes enough alcohol, wits, common sense and reasonable behavior go on hiatus. Now, all the people who I found intolerable and idiotic just hours prior, became interesting and entertaining. It is really quite incredible what enough beer does to inhibitions and boundaries. Drinking beer with my fellow Marines rather than resenting them for it, changed everything.

One guy said, "Wow, you're from Seattle?! What's that like?"

"Actually, no, I'm not from Seattle. I grew up North of Seattle in a town called Arlington..."

The guy said, "Arlington? Like the cemetery?"

Try explaining geography of Washington State to a person who has not only never been there but has likely never heard of anything outside of Seattle or Mount St. Helens and is drunk sometime. The guy literally thought I was describing Southeast Alaska when I said, "North of Seattle." I had to tell him, and others over and over so many times that there was much more to Washington State than Seattle. Finally, after so many times explaining it and so many drinks of my own, I just started telling people I was from Seattle.

To drink beer as a new Marine is like drinking an elixir that grants rite of passage and official membership into the Corps. The only thing I lacked was a Marine tattoo.

***

Like anyone young and new to drinking, my experience was an exercise in learning my limitations and going way beyond them. For example, common behavior on a night in the barracks involved keeping count of how many each of us had consumed, like a competition. Before long, normal routine was 8-12 beers a night for me. Followed in the morning by a trip to the chow hall for food to absorb the hangover.

The whole lot of us would still be to work on time every morning, learning how to work on aircraft. Mostly however, new guys got put on tow crews and wash crews. Cobras and Hueys lack wheels, so hydraulically pumped up wheels get attached to skids and a tow vehicle moves aircraft around the flight line, hangars and wash racks. The work is tedious and hot, I hated it. Wash rack wasn't much more pleasant, though you could at least cool off a little on hot days. My Sergeants likely sensed my disdain for the tasks, as I ended up on those details a lot. In fact one week we were behind on washes, so a crew was assembled to come in on Saturday to get caught up. I was of course on that detail. The wash crew that day worked until lunch, we all walked up to the closest E-Club to down several pitchers of beer before finishing out the day.

I would call home frequently in the first few years, three to five times a week was not unusual. Even after I started drinking with the guys regularly, I still despised my mom for her drinking. I was very curt with my greetings when mom answered the phone, there was zero desire on my behalf to let her have details about my life and thus be emotionally attached. I realized, even then, that my mind was reasoning comparisons between mom and me regarding alcohol in our lives. We were both making choices to drink I reasoned. In her case she drank alone and chose to make her drinking a priority over family. In my case, I didn't particularly enjoy the process of drinking, so the choice I made was that I knew it enabled me to fit into the Marine culture.

Inevitably one of my fellow Marines finally said the magic words that set me off into rage almost immediately every time I heard them. One of my brothers said, "I can't help that I like to drink so much, my dad was an alcoholic, so I inherited it. I have to drink."

The idea of inheriting alcoholism was always absurd to me, especially when someone referred to it as a disease. I would argue until blue in the face about how wrong that thinking was. For those who labeled alcoholism as a disease I would say something smart like, "Oh really? Well let's call the CDC and report an outbreak!" For the people that told me it was inherited I would say, "Well my mom drinks, her dad drinks and I only do so around you. When I'm alone I hate to drink, so how did I inherit anything?"

I hated the idea of being compared to my mom or have suggestions made that we had anything in common. Hated it.

***

After being in the fleet for a few months, I talked to the Gunny about ROTC. I asked the Gunny if he would give me guidance and help me through the hoops. Gunny said, "First learn your job and how to be a good Marine, then we'll talk about it."

I became dejected. I thought that the Marine Corps had no intention of ever letting me strive for what I dreamed about. I thought the Corps was selfish. I resented the NCOs, Gunny and Officers. I resented my parents for their fighting and my mom for her ridiculous need to be drunk. I resented my recruiter and the officer who interviewed me for ROTC while in high school. I resented all the people who said they would stay in touch yet forgot about me once I was out of mind. The only person I didn't resent, was myself.

Late in 1995 the Gunfighters rotated to Okinawa for my first deployment.

As we worked closer to the actual deploy date I kept kicking myself for dropping that second year of Japanese. I had asked the teacher and counselor, "When will I ever be in Japan?" Well there I was, along with the rest of the squadron, packing for the six-month deployment. We were briefed on customs and courtesies, what types of places to avoid and current events. Specifically, we were warned about local Okinawan sentiment toward Marines and sailors since two Marines and one sailor had just gang raped a minor Okinawan girl. The command went as far as to advise we spend most of our liberty on base and to avoid the local communities.

That was never going to happen. Like most of my fellow Marines, while I wasn't necessarily thrilled about the trip, I wanted to make the most of it. I wanted to see sites from the battle for the island in 1945. I wanted to see castles. I wanted to try local cuisine. Really, I just wanted to live the experience and do some sightseeing.

I wound up doing all of those things, though what I ended up doing most nights was drinking at the bar just outside the front gate. A Corporal from my shop introduced me to the place and I graduated to hard liquor. The bar had this assortment of drinks to try that they called a "bridge." If you made it through the whole series of drinks, there was some kind of reward. I don't recall what it was and I never came remotely close. I just remember how profanely strong the drinks were and how my head swam trying to trek up the steep hill back to the barracks.

One particular night I made an attempt at the bridge on a work night. I of course failed and do not remember how I made it back to the barracks. I do remember barely making it to the hangar on time the next morning and the job our Airframe Sergeant assigned me that day. He obviously knew I had drank heavily the night before, and the Sergeant punished me as only a Sergeant can, informally. For starters he told me to get my cranial on. (Cranials are flight line head gear with plastic protection and noise suppression. They're very hot, sweaty and uncomfortable if worn for long periods of time.) So I put the cranial on. My job that day was to replace the top windscreen (windshield) on a Cobra. Those things are a bear to replace. They take all day because they never fit exactly right out of the box and require lots of shaving and working of hole alignment for the attaching hardware. I was up there all day, where I perspired profusely and nearly got sick. Another word was never said to me about showing up to work so badly hung over, and I never did it again.

A vast majority of my correspondence with home while in Okinawa was via letters. Email wasn't prevalent yet and phone calls were made, albeit sparingly. With hearing my dad's voice so infrequently and my mom's voice even less, I didn't focus much on my parents. Loosely speaking that trip to Okinawa was akin to Marine Boot Camp, very little contact with loved ones and emphasized focus on our mission. I turned 20 while in Okinawa that first time, and still keep to this day a letter my dad wrote for my birthday. In the letter he talks about how proud they are of the man I've become. At the time I felt like a huge fraud. My whole reason for being a Marine was to get away from an alcoholic, yet there I was drinking frequently with the guys. I knew that for the most part I did so to fit in, though I was very conflicted. I felt like a total hypocrite.

Chapter 17

In the spring of 1996 the Gunfighters rotated back stateside. Landing on American soil after a deployment was such a surreal feeling. Granted, it's not like we were fighting a war at the time, but we were still in a foreign country and the feeling of euphoria upon touching home soil cannot be understated. The whole plane cheered when the captain came over the intercom and said, "Welcome Home."

For over a year I was part of a group of new Marines to report to the squadron and none reported while we were deployed. So I was the new guy for a quite a long time. New guys got stuck on details that sucked the most. I would imagine it was that way everywhere in the military, though I still contend to this day that Marine Sergeants are the most creative in ways of making young Marines miserable. They are really savants at making Marines hate life, it really ought to be recognized as art.

A few months after our return I made Corporal, finally I was an NCO. Becoming an NCO in the Corps is really a pride point for any Marine. For starters you get to wear the iconic blood stripe on dress pants. More importantly, it means you aren't the boot anymore. Upon our return a new group of Marines started trickling into our squadron, and life for me improved some. I was finally above *somebody* in the pecking order.

Along with my new promotion, the Gunny also got me a new assignment. I was sent over to phase crew. For the people reading this who aren't sure what a phase crew is, I'll explain. Aircraft flight hours are diligently tracked, and there is a reason for it. There are certain benchmarks in the life of an airframe where certain inspections and preventative/restorative maintenance need to be done. It's usually measured by hundreds of hours. Well phase crew is a team of Marines representing each of the mechanical disciplines within the squadron who are responsible for doing this maintenance. It is not flight line work, it is much more in depth than daily maintenance. In our case there was a Gunny over us and one or two Marines from each shop to accomplish the inspection. The aircraft is brought into the hangar and stripped down as far as it needs to be to accomplish whatever maintenance needed to happen. A typical stay for an aircraft was at a minimum, several days if the airframe is in great shape. Older airframes that have issues could be out of the flight schedule for weeks.

I mention phase crew in my story for two reasons. First, the experience was my first real involved exposure to other mechanical disciplines. The time really opened my eyes to the process of maintaining aircraft outside of my little world. Timing was really excellent for this because I had really buckled down upon getting Corporal and wanted to know my job at the highest levels and test for CDI. CDI is Collateral Duty Inspector or in civilian terms Quality Assurance. Essentially what that meant for me was the responsibility of checking the work of other Marines and signing off on an aircraft as safe for flight from the airframe perspective. Learning about the other systems really enhanced my appreciation for working together to get an aircraft ready for flight and taught me a healthy dose of respect for working with the other disciplines. Secondly, I made one really amazing lifelong friend in phase crew, David McIntosh, known as Mac.

The more I worked with Mac the more I really liked him. Like me, he was a small-town guy, though he grew up in small town West Illinois. We had some interesting similarities regarding family dysfunction which I won't go into. What I will say about it is, I trusted Mac because he understood me.

Around that time I had curtailed my drinking significantly. For starters, I had real aspirations and goals for the first time since high school, I desperately wanted to be an inspector. Additionally, I had really started to settle and felt like I belonged. I had carved out my identity and knew what I wanted to be. I still drank, though I was more selective. Most of the drinking I did was in the barracks room with my roommate Chad or with Mac. Mostly we just kicked back with some beer and spent hours talking about life and what we wanted from it. In those two Marines I found new family, family that I chose. With them I felt safe for the first time in my life to open up about my mom. I told them how I idolized my dad and hated my mom for being an alcoholic burden. Chad and Mac were judgement free, they just listened, gave me empathy and acceptance. With them I was safe to say how little I really liked drinking and only did it because it is the default culture of Marine Corps life. I told them how much I felt like a fraud and a hypocrite. They didn't pressure me to drink nor did they encourage me not to. With those two guys it was just acceptance.

For a time late in 1996 and early 1997 I cut even further back on drinking. I would have a few over the weekend, but seldom to the point of excess. In fact for my 21st birthday I didn't even have a drink at all. I went to a small beachside coffee place with another buddy and listened to live music.

I called home that night to talk to my dad for my birthday and of course mom answered the phone. She'd already been partying for me. I tried to be tolerant and have a conversation with her, but I could only take repeated words and slurs for so long before getting agitated. Mom asked if I was celebrating my 21st birthday with drinks. I said, "No mom. I can find other ways to celebrate, you should try it." Mom didn't get mad, she got quiet. She told me she was putting dad on the phone. In the moment I remember feeling empowered. I had experienced significant alcohol consumption and was powerful enough mentally to make the decision for how big a role alcohol played in my life. I had proven to myself that alcohol consumption was a choice, and since it was a choice mom received no empathy from me.

***

By fall of 1997 it was time once again for the Gunfighters to go to Okinawa. Everything about the second trip felt different though. This time I was an NCO, Marines who hadn't been deployed would pick my brain about what to expect. This time I was going as a CDI. This time I would be in the mix for a leadership role. Mac was going to be my roommate and for several months of our deployment he was on a MEU (Marine Expeditionary Unit) float. What his MEU meant for me, was a room to myself for a big chunk of time.

Another Marine named Brian and I were assigned leadership for the night shift. What I loved about night shift was the freedom of it. At shift change either Brian or I would attend a maintenance meeting. At the meeting, representatives from each shop are present. The Marine leading the meeting was usually a Gunny or Staff Sergeant, he would go through the aircraft one by one and identify which issues the aircraft had mechanically and assign priorities for the work to be done. It was up to Brian and I to assemble maintenance teams to get those jobs done and then check the work for quality. Nobody went home until maintenance had achieved readiness on enough aircraft for flight operations the next day. Sometimes we even had operations at night which led to some long nights. So while Brian and I had enormous latitude and autonomy in our lives, we also worked the longest hours.

The schedule also helped keep me out of barracks parties during the week.

Brian and I made a good team. We really kept a good balance of utilizing the strengths of the more adept Marines in our shop to get the more complex or high pressure jobs done while also training up the new Marines. On slower nights we rotated our men and women through early quitting times to get them some extra liberty. Those types of small gestures really kept morale up on their first deployment.

On January 1st, 1998 I was promoted to Sergeant. Attaining the rank of Sergeant in the Marine Corps was really an iconic life achievement. I had never felt more like a Marine than I did the first time one of my Marines called me Sergeant. Sergeants are the backbone of the Marine Corps, anybody will tell you that. What it meant for me? It was a pinnacle moment in pride. Sure other promotions were possible, but Sergeants were the hands-on leaders. I was important to the Corps now. I was counted on by officers and those above me to lead Marines. Perhaps not like a father to those Marines who worked for me, but more like a big brother. I wanted to be the Marine they looked up to. I wanted my Marines to count on me. I needed to set an example.

That night, we partied. We partied a lot. Chad, Brian and I filled a full-size refrigerator with Budweiser, I mean literally filled. There was nothing else in it. Then we reveled late into the night until it was morning.

***

The real challenge of leadership is not in the success of each day as a Marine, it comes in the failures of those who are under your charge. A few weeks after getting Sergeant chevrons pinned on, our Gunny came to Brian and me. One of our Marines had been caught shoplifting from the exchange at another base nearby. Once back in our custody the responsibility of disciplining the young Marine was delegated to us. I had never been so angry with a fellow Marine before or since. As a young man and young Marine, you know that Marines do some stupid things. Stealing from a store though? We made that Private's life total hell for that weekend and many following weeks to come. White glove room inspections, full uniform inspections and more shit details than I could count. A very long time passed before that Private was no longer the subject of my ire.

***

Aside from promotion night, I really refrained from heavy drinking on the second Okinawa trip. Oh Mac and I had a handful of cold ones from time to time, but I had really mellowed out. I did not go to that bar off base one time on the second trip and only went to the E-club a handful of times, and even then mostly because it was new and had good food. I only called home a handful of times and mom sent me and the guys cookies for Christmas that trip. In retrospect, that deployment was awesome. I really found my place in the Corps and it felt amazing to feel needed and important. What made it better was doing my part to pass on the legacy of what it meant to train Marines who were deployed for the first time and to be their Sergeant. What did I need to drink for?

1998 was a strange year of uncertainty at HMLA-369. Shortly after getting back stateside some things were happening on the world scale that affected us. For a period of time we were the "quick response" or "ready" unit. What that meant was that if 3rd Marine Air Wing needed to send a light attack squadron somewhere on short notice, we were it. Well as it turns out a lot happened in 1998.

Embassy bombings in Kenya and Tanzania by Osama bin Laden and Al Qaeda. President Bill
Clinton responds with cruise missiles, we were advised to be ready.

Sadaam Hussein violating no-fly zones. We were advised to be ready.

Kosovo.

For me at least, the most difficult part of those situations was uncertainty. Did I want to go to Iraq or Afghanistan in 1998? Not particularly. Though if it was to be done, I was of the mindset that we just go already!

I never did deploy for combat as a United States Marine.

After we were home a few months I was put in charge of the Corrosion Control division. Other shops had to send me one Marine each for corrosion prevention and minor paint repairs. I think those Marines would agree that to one degree or another they were kind of being "punished" by their shops. For whatever the reason was, those Marines were sent to me, I did not care. I took care of my Marines. Those men and women loved working for me, loved it. They have all told me so, I have in fact been told some flattering words by each of them, even the ones who gave me a few problems here and there. I am still in contact today with most of them.

As a Sergeant, I was eligible to move off base, and I did. So that was my first experience with apartments and real-world adult responsibilities like rent and groceries. I drank very sparingly, usually just when a few of my Marines would visit. By that time Chad had moved on to another base in California so his visits were rare. Mac and I would go out from time to time to have a beer wherever country music was played and shoot some billiards. He had found some other interests around that time so his visits to just sit and sip some suds while we chatted became much scarcer.

I had a land line and huge phone bill. Back in 1998/1999 I don't recall anybody having cell phones. It was just land lines with terrible long-distance packages. The bills I got from calling home to talk with dad were outrageous. *Several hundred dollars!*

Sadly, I was compelled to transfer out of the Gunfighters by the end of summer in 1999. They were going back to Okinawa and there was not enough time on my enlistment to go with. I received orders for the training squadron, HMT-

303. I was sad to leave my squadron. I loved being a Gunfighter. Even on the days when I didn't care for the Corps, I was born to be a Gunfighter. Part of me is still a Gunfighter.

***

I called home on the night before I reported to the new squadron to talk to my dad. Whenever I found myself in a spot where I needed a pickup or advice, dad was my go-to guy. With the new squadron I would have to prove myself all over again. To them, I was nobody, just some transfer. I wouldn't even be a CDI anymore, for that I would have to test all over. All of these negative scenarios in my head, all of these worries and dread over the unknown.

Mom answered the phone and I tried to talk to her.

"Hey mom. I'm going to the new squadron tomorrow. I'm worried."

Mom, "What? Why do you have to go? When will you be back?"

(Sighing because yet again I'm at a crossroads in life where some sober words of encouragement from my mother and a sliver of emotional support was probably all I actually needed.) "Mom, I'm not *going* anywhere. Just down the flight line to a different hangar, a different squadron."

Mom, "Why?"

Me, "Because my old unit is going to Okinawa, and I can't go."

Slurring and agitated, mom, "Why can't you go?"

Pissed off now, me, "Because mom, my enlistment is almost up. Put dad on the phone please."

Mom, "I don't understand."

Me, "Yeah because you're drunk. Just put dad on the phone."

Mom, "He's not home yet."

Me, "Fine, I'll just call back. Good bye."

***

HMT-303 welcomed me with open arms. They were actually pretty awesome. There was a Captain over the airframe division who I really liked, Captain Long. Captain Long was not some new Lieutenant just learning to fly, he was a good officer who knew how to lead. There was also an amazing Staff Sergeant there, Staff Sergeant V.

My new leadership helped me get through hoops and get re-certified as a CDI pretty quick and then asked if I would be willing to run the night shift with Staff Sergeant V. I said of course, that I preferred the night shift. Then Captain Long had the re-enlistment talk with me.

Captain, "What's your interest level in reenlisting?"

Me, "Well honestly I don't think I'd like to. I'm ready for a change. If I wanted to stay in I'd be with the Gunfighters."

Captain, "Fair enough. Anything I can say or do to persuade you otherwise?"

Me, "If you could arrange for me to do it on Iwo Jima, on top of Mount Suribachi, then I would say yes."

Laughing, Captain, "I don't think so."

Shrugging, Me, "Ok, I'll just get out then."

That was it. No more pressure or judgement. I just kept coming to work and doing my very best to keep aircraft safely flying and leading Marines.

Staff Sergeant V was great to work with. He obviously had me outranked, but we ran things as a team. I learned a lot from him about leadership, specifically in regard to troop welfare and selflessness. He was one of the purest most natural leaders I have ever met. Below is an example of the kind of man he was, a letter to my parents:

To the parents of Sgt. Matthew Whittington

Let me be the first to tell you about Sgt Whittington's superior performance while stationed with Marine Helicopter Training Squadron 303. During the past few months that I have been with the squadron, he has shown to me that he is willing to take on the challenge and responsibilities embodied in the Marine Corps like no other. He has also shown to me the professionalism which most other military branches of service and civilian company employees lack.

Working as an airframe mechanic in the Marine Corps Air Wing takes a lot of dedication and creativity. Knowing the structure of the two helicopters we work on can be very stressful. From removing a simple panel to reconstructing an entire section, it's all taken with the utmost dedication. As an airframer, we also have the responsibility of maintaining the hydraulic flight control system. Each day, our pilots and their crewmembers depend on us to ensure that the plane they are flying (excuse the phrase) doesn't fall to pieces in mid-flight. I have seen your son at work, and I would like to say that I am very impressed, as you should be. He has worked very hard and has come a long way since he had graduated from recruit training and his tech schools to accomplish what he has today.

During our time working together on the same shift, I have been most fortunate to have him along my side. He has been one of the most resourceful and dedicated individuals who I have crossed paths with. With only a short time remaining on his military contract, he still carries with him the responsibility needed to accomplish a mission. A characteristic that many "short-time" Marines care not to have. As one of the best Collateral Duties Inspectors I have worked with, his expertise and leadership will be greatly missed. I wish him the best of luck in the future.

As a personal note to you, I see your son as not only one of my troops, but as one of my family members. I assure you that I will to the best of my knowledge and ability, take him under my wing and assist him with any problems he might encounter. The only thing I ask from you, his parents, is at any given time, day or night, give him a call of recognition and encouragement. Troop moral is my number two (safety being number one) objective in the Marine Corps.

Semper Fidelis

V
SSGT/USMC

Dad of course responded as only he could:

SSGT V.

We enjoyed reading your letter very much. It's very flattering that you would take the time and effort to let us know how special our son is! Some of the qualities that you mentioned, like superior performance, challenges, responsibilities, dedication and pride lead us to believe that you have made a mistake. The reason why we believe this is because our Matthew is a self-centered, hard-headed, cocky and arrogant young man. He is a beer drinking, whore chasing, party animal. The only way he made it through high school was by snitching, brown nosing, sucking up and kissing ass.

Actually SSGT V, we are putting you on. Thank you very much for being there. We love our son very much and we are glad that Matthew has such great friends who care for him. The day that Matthew left our home for the Marines was the saddest day of our lives. We cried and missed him greatly. We feared for our son and prayed daily that he stay out of harms way. After all, now he was out and on his own far from home. It eases our minds that we can rely on outstanding young men such as yourself to look out for our son. We salute you and are proud of you as well.

Matthew has always been self-motivated, regimented and disciplined young man. He sets goals and stays on tasks. He graduated high school an honor graduate. His name is on a banner in the high school gym to testify to his accomplishments. He has only done in the Marines what he has always done, and that is to take pride in himself and always remember who you are and where you come from. Matthew looks and listens very well and we are very proud.

From the time Matthew was a baby, his attention would turn to the sky every time the roar of an airplane would pass overhead. He would drag me out to every airshow possible. He would spend hours hanging out at flight operations to get autographs and talk to pilots. His dream is to get his ride in a gunship before separation. His time grows short and his dream of getting that ride now dims. If you can help Matthew live his dream, he would surely reward you by keeping the memories dear to him forever.

We are going to close now by wishing you and yours nothing but the best. May God bless you and keep you from harms way. Thanks again.

Sincerely,

Frank Whittington
Janet Whittington

When Staff Sergeant V received that letter back, I did not know the exchange of correspondence had taken place. He forwarded copies of the letters up the chain to the commanding officer through Captain Long, and the flight was scheduled. Only then was I pulled in and told what had happened. Staff Sergeant V showed me the letters. Both letters touched me, and the one from my parents was signed "Frank and Janet" but those were my dad's words. I loved him for it. With one sheet of paper, an envelope and a stamp he had done everything within his power to get me in that Cobra.

I had not quite reached my goal of becoming a fighter pilot, but for one day, at least I flew. Two hours and five minutes of front seat Super Cobra flight time, the most exhilarating experience of my life. I did not just sit in the seat, for short periods of time Captain Long gave me the stick. I flew that Cobra.

As for my dad's claim that I would reward them by holding the memory dear, I did and still do.

On Memorial Day weekend 2000, I used the rest of my leave and separated a month early from active duty United States Marine Corps. My official service ended June 26, 2000. I was honorably discharged as a Sergeant.

To this day I still refer to myself as:

A Marine Corps Sergeant

And

Gunfighter

Part 2

"The weak can never forgive. Forgiveness is the attribute of the strong." - Mahatma Gandhi

Chapter 18

I didn't have a job lined up.

I didn't have a residence in mind.

I didn't have a plan for what came next at all.

First priority was to find a place to live. An old friend flew down to Southern California to split driving duties on my trip home, JD. Somewhere along the way we agreed that sharing an apartment would be the ideal way to go. During the weeks it took for the two of us to find a place, I had to stay with my parents. Now, I loved my dad and was happy to be home, but the idea of living with them again was not at all what I wanted.

I had been gone for six years, in that time I had grown accustomed to independence and control over my residence.

In the first days sitting in the house I grew up in, all I could think about was moving into my own place. Staying there didn't feel right, it felt like going backwards. Mom was as bad as ever with her drinking. She would just sit there with a huge smile on her face just looking at me. I'm sure she was happy, but her just sitting there staring at me was freaking me out.

I would say, "Mom, what are you looking at me like that for?"

She would say, "Oh no reason."

Then I just rolled my eyes before getting up and walking away.

In the short few weeks I was there, mom was completely off the deep end intoxicated every single night. No meaningful conversations about life took place. No profound revelations or advice about what I should do with my life happened. I felt a great emptiness. Obviously there would be no relationship as an adult now that I was home, certainly even less involvement or interest even from when I lived under the roof as a minor.

What did I expect? I knew she hadn't quit drinking in the six years I was gone. It seemed the only variable that had changed was how much everyone else cared. Even my dad seemed more apathetic about her addiction, like he had just broken and accepted her.

Why did something that was unlikely to change bother me so much? After all, my stay would be brief and she wasn't my problem. I've put a lot of reflective thought into that moment over the years and have come up with a couple points of interest.

First, observing the changes in my dad after six years absent was depressing. It appeared to me that he had just given up hope of ever having a sober wife. A wife who was attentive and engaging. Given up on having present a person, who when sober, was warm and loving. Rather, he just appeared to concede all. Dad appeared to have accepted that he would share the rest of his life with a drunk.

Secondly, I for one craved to have a mother. I desperately wanted a mom who I could confide in regarding my goals and desires for the rest of my life. A mom who could provide me with thoughtful and meaningful counsel. I had deprived myself female companionship while in the Corps. I knew going forward that having a family in my life was important. Finding someone to share my life with would be a huge priority. Sure, I talked with my dad about a lot of things, this was one of those things I wanted to have my mom around for.

***

By the end of June 2000, I was in my first apartment since leaving the Marines. I had also found my first job since getting out, an entry level airplane mechanic with a small business out of Paine Field, Everett. I was only making $12 an hour.

Within a few months I met someone who would prove to be very important in influencing my maturity and therefore shape the man I have become, Alison.

When I met Alison, she was going through a divorce. We had a very strong chemistry, there were subtle similarities that drew us to one another. Alison's focus was mostly about proving to herself that she was capable of independence. I guess it would be fair to say that she was in the midst of finding herself. She was the complete opposite of "damsel in distress". Alison was finding empowerment in her life. Her strength spoke to me.

Alison and I dated for a few months before we were ready for the "meet the parents" visits. I dreaded introducing her to my parents. My fear had everything to do with thinking she might judge my character differently after meeting my mom. Alison believed that how a man treated his mom was a good indicator for how he would be as a spouse. With that knowledge in mind, I really thought my new relationship was in trouble.

Rather than attempting to hide the truth, I elected to take the full disclosure and honesty route. Days before Alison was to meet my parents I started preparing her for my mom by giving her the full background on what it was like growing up with an alcoholic. Further, I tried to explain to her my feelings of anger and resentment toward my mom. I detailed to Alison that issues between mom and I were unique and did not project on other women.

On the way to my parent's house with Alison, I was completely stressed out. In my mind I could envision arriving only to find my mom stupid drunk. I knew that no amount of will power could give me the strength to ignore my anger and keep the edge from my words. I really liked Alison, I didn't know if we would get married or where the relationship would end up going forward. What I did know is that I really liked her, and this was the first time I had gone so far in bringing someone home to meet the parents.

With small relief I knew almost immediately upon arrival that mom had tried to keep her drinking in check. She was not outrageously drunk as I had feared she might be. Mom had been drinking though. By her demeanor and body language, I figured she'd only been at it an hour or two. Enough for me to notice, yet not enough to lose basic communication skills with non-drunks. I chalked it up to a small victory for me. Mom had shown some restraint, for that much I was thankful.

Mom did continue drinking during our visit. Once she started sneaking off for periods of time to drink, I knew the time for our departure was drawing near. I had no intention of exposing Alison to a completely inebriated mom on the very first visit. I came up with an excuse to leave.

Alison asked, "Are you sure we need to leave, we could stay a bit longer."

I said, "Yep. We need to go."

Dad looked a little bummed that I had cut the visit short, though I'm sure he knew why. Mom looked surprised and a little hurt that I was calling it a night, I'm sure she had no idea why. While I was thankful that she was reasonably engaged and pleasant, I knew it was only a matter of time before moods changed. Once she hit a certain point, sweet Janet would become obnoxious drunk Janet.

A few miles down the road, Alison asked if I was ok. I told her the truth. I told her that while I was fine, the day was going to trend badly if we stayed much longer. Alison seemed genuinely interested and concerned.

Alison, "What do you mean the day was starting to go badly?"

Me, "I'm not sure if you would notice, but my mom was in and out of our conversations. The reason for that was she was sneaking off for drinks."

Alison, "She seemed very nice, everybody was very nice."

Me, "Did you grow up with an alcoholic parent?"

Alison, "Well, not really so much growing up. Both of my parents drink now though."

Me, "I'm sorry, it may be hard to understand if you didn't grow up with it."

Alison, "Try me."

Me, "I know my mom seems very sweet and nice. She will reach a point though where she turns obnoxious and nasty."

A few moments passed by where I was trying to keep the red from my face and Alison reflected.

Alison, "I think you might be too hard on your mom. We really need to learn to forgive our parents. They do the best they can. Your mom is an alcoholic, it's a disease, and she can't help it."

I know Alison meant well, but forgiveness for her "disease" was more than I could handle. I did not yell; my speech did become more assertive though.

Me, "It's not a disease. Alcoholism is a choice. It's a choice. If it were a disease, then I would be a hopeless drunk. Her dad was a drunk, my mom is a drunk, so why am I not? Because it's a choice. This was important to me, I have never brought anyone home, you're the first. Yet, she still could not leave the beer alone. That beer did not open itself, she chose to open it and she chose to drink it. Choice."

A few minutes passed by. I felt I had stopped just short of scolding Alison, and I certainly used a great deal of restraint to not yell out of frustration.

Some time passed by in silence before anybody said anything.

Alison, "I had a good time."

How I did not break down and cry, I will never know.

Chapter 19

Alison and I were still dating when the calendar turned over to 2001. The topic of marriage was discussed, while she wasn't totally closed to the idea, Alison said she needed a few years. She asked that I not propose to her until she told me she was ready. Having the ability to ask when I wanted taken wasn't easy, but I really didn't want to lose her from my life. Months after that she had a surgery that would prevent her from ever having another child that hit me hard too. I wanted kids. I wanted the opportunity to prove to myself that I could raise children, I thought I would be an amazing husband and father.

The day of the surgery Alison went through to prevent future children, we had a conversation.

Alison, "Matt, as you know, I don't want any more kids. One is enough. I know you want kids. Does this need to be the end?"

I didn't speak for a moment. I knew I wanted kids. I also knew that I loved Alison. I knew in that split second I had to give up one or the other.

Me, "I want you."

Alison, "I know you do. I don't want to lose you, but I want to be fair to you. This is your chance."

Another moment of reflection. That conversation had to be very hard on Alison, yet in a strange way, the strength with which she composed herself was one of the very qualities that made her so special.

Me, "I'm sure. I want you."

I wasn't sure. I lied. I lied to Alison, and I lied to myself. I think she knew it.

***

As the next few years passed I thought less often about having kids, though it never left my mind completely. I did the best I could to get my daddy fill through Alison's daughter. Through no fault of the child however, I never felt like a dad. Alison and her ex-husband shared custody and I was really more of a third wheel. Alison and I dated until one day in early 2004, she sat down next to me and said, "I'm ready. Now, are you sure you don't want to have kids?"

In a moment that may have seemed like minutes, but in reality was just a few seconds I made the decision, again, to lie.

I told her, "Yes, I'm sure. I really have all I need with you and your daughter."

We planned for the wedding to take place at her parent's house on Lake Ki in Washington State. The plan was for the wedding to be on the smaller side of large, I believe our guest list was about 35-50 people.

In the months leading up to the big day, we paid a visit to a cousin I grew up with. She and her family lived in Eastern Washington. During my Marine Corps years, they lived in

Lake Havasu City, Arizona where I would visit on longer weekends. I visited often enough that I held all their kids as babies and played with them as toddlers. They were a big part of my life and were there for me as family while everyone else was so far away. During the visit before the wedding my cousin pulled me aside and asked if I was sure about spending the rest of my life without kids. My cousin said she and her husband had talked several times about how they thought I would be a terrific father. While they thought the world of Alison, she just wanted to check and make sure I had really thought things through.

I told her I had, which was the truth. Yet, I lied once more about being ok with no kids.

I talked to my dad. Dad said how much he wished I could have kids. I reminded him that both my brother and sister gave him grand kids and that he was gaining a ten-year-old step granddaughter.

The truth is, by the time our wedding day was imminent, I was sick of thinking about kids. I was sick of everyone second guessing me. I was tired of people warning Alison about marrying me and vice versa. Fact was, I truly loved her. There were so many redeeming qualities that she brought to life that I weighed them with more favor than the uncertainty of starting over and hoping I found someone compatible with me who wanted to start a family. I *knew* I loved her, I did *not know* that starting over would be better or even possible.

So within days of the wedding I called home to chat with dad about the rehearsal dinner, mom answered the phone, and of course she was obnoxiously drunk.

Mom, "Matt, are you excited for your wedding?"

Me, "Yes mom, is dad home?"

Mom, "He'll be home soon. Matt, I really wish you and Alison would have some kids."

Maybe I was already agitated to be stuck on the phone with Janet the drunk or maybe I was just sick of everyone telling me what I should want. In that moment, I had hit the point of never wanting to discuss kids again. I was sick of the topic. I'm sure she meant well and thought she was looking out for my happiness, but I snapped.

Me, "Mom. I'm not having any kids. Do you understand me? No kids! It is not about what you wish for or what you want, this is about what I want. I want Alison. Be happy for me."

Mom, "Matthew…"

Me, "No mom. Stop. Just tell dad I called please."

I hung up the phone. I didn't feel bad for raising my voice to her. I remember thinking that if she cared enough to have a conversation of this importance, then she could call me sober and we'd have a thoughtful chat. I was not going to have a debate with a drunk, and that was the end of it.

Early morning July 10, 2004 I got a call from Alison, she had stayed with her sister the night before the wedding. The whole thing where you're not supposed to see each other. She was upset and on the edge of losing her composure.

She asked me to meet her at Harborview Medical Center in Seattle, the area's premier trauma unit. I asked what was wrong, and she said, "Just meet me there, fast!" Before I could get out of the house she called back and told me to change my destination from the hospital to her parent's house.

I said, "Alison, what's wrong? What has happened?!"

Alison, "The house caught fire, dad got out, mom didn't. They went to airlift her, but she died before getting there. Hurry please, speed!"

***

A few weeks after the fire and memorial services, Alison pulled me aside. She said, "You need to forgive your mom."

I looked at her, knowing that my reaction could very well cause our wedding to never be rescheduled, knowing that this woman who had just lost her mother wanted to see me have a positive and lasting relationship with mine. After a moment I said softly, "I'm sorry, I can't. The pain is too much."

The look on Alison's face was pained, yet thoughtful, "Forgive your parents for your upbringing, they did the best they could."

***

Nearly four months after the tragic loss of Alison's mother, we married in a small ceremony on Lake Ki. My parents were there along with Alison's father and two of Alison's friends; one as maid of honor and one to take pictures. In the pictures, a lump was visible on the side of my dad's neck. Upon returning from the honeymoon, my dad told me he had terminal cancer.

When my dad called to give me the news, I was working an outside sales job for Zep Manufacturing. That day my sales manager was riding along, giving tips and advice for how to show products. The two of us were sitting in a parking lot somewhere when the call came. I welled up with tears as my dad spoke.

"Metastatic ... aggressive ... throat ... six months ..."

Those were the only words I heard. Somewhere in that one-sided talk he also mentioned treatment and what a best-case scenario would be if things moved slowly. I sat there dumbfounded, nodding my head at the cell phone as he spoke (as if he could see me nodding). I tried very hard to not cry in front of my new boss. His name was Mike. Mike asked if I wanted to talk about the phone call, so I gave him enough details to understand. Mike desperately wanted to have a great sales day, and I told him I would carry on. Instead he said, "Let's go to lunch."

At lunch I confided in Mike as if he were a lifelong friend. I told him I was scared. I told him that I had serious doubts that my dad would receive the attention he needed to survive. When pressed I told him my mom was an awful drunk and I had no faith in her ability to take care of my sick father. I told Mike that my father was likely to die very soon, and that he was my role model.

Mike told me to go home.

Talking that night to Alison about all my thoughts and fears, she wondered aloud if maybe the adversity would be enough to sober my mom up.

It was not.

While my dad went through chemotherapy and radiation, mom continued to drink. Even the threat of losing her husband was not enough to incentivize sobriety. Fortunately for the family my sister lived very close and was able to help dad out quite a bit. My sister helped care for him at home a lot and helped with many appointments. I was very thankful for her help, especially since I had just started a new job and lived nearly two hours away.

What little halfhearted effort at forgiveness I considered making regarding my mom quickly evaporated. In reality the opposite effect manifested, I became much angrier. Every time I spoke to my dad he seemed to sound very sick and drained. Dad didn't want to talk on the phone, from sound alone things seemed to be going very poorly. Yet, as worlds were falling apart throughout the family, mom just kept on drinking. I already couldn't forgive her absence as a mother, now she seemed to be checking out as a wife too.

Fight or flight. It's real. You either fight for what you love or you run away. In my mind, mom had resigned herself to his death and left him to it. From what information I was able to get, she had chosen, flight. Running away, even further into the abyss of alcohol addiction.

Unforgiveable.

***

Radiation and chemotherapy failed.

My dad was given two books. The first book was a bible I had carried with me throughout my service. I hadn't been nor was I a devout, church attending Christian. Yet, somehow that bible had managed to stay in my possession for several years. I wrote in the front of that bible that I had carried it for many years and hoped it would help him, then I gave it to my dad.

I would say that prior to cancer my father was spiritual, yet I don't recall him identifying strongly with religion or attending church frequently. As a child I found my dad to be of high moral character, generally empathetic and overall he was concerned about being a good citizen. He and my mother had some differences when it came to how to worship, so I believe as a result we were kind of left to our own as kids to find our spiritual paths. I would characterize my view at the time as 'God pays more attention to acts than he does chapel attendance.'

The second book my dad had at the time was, *The Cure for All Cancers* by Hulda Clark. Essentially, how that book claims to cure cancer is through diet and habits. For example certain kinds of foods, from certain places, cooked in a certain ways and lacking preservatives. Minutia up to what types of utensils are used and their composition play a role. The entire premise seemed a little silly to me.

Dad left his home to go stay with a sister who introduced him to the book. With her help, he was able to absorb the expense and effort of undergoing those dietary changes the book outlined. Doing so was a full-time job and took a great deal of effort and dedication.

Then, an amazing thing happened. Dad started getting better.

In fact, his health improved so much that the cancer not only went into remission, it disappeared from his body!

What at one time was a draconian countdown to the loss of my father, became a miraculous recovery. The doctors who months prior had prognosticated imminent death, had to admit that they were not always right, that my dad would live past those six months after all.

Without the tireless work of my aunt and sister, that recovery would not have been possible. They worked very hard with negligible affirmation toward the goal of recovery where scores of others, including my dad's medical team, would have just given up. Of course the fierce perseverance and refusal to give up within my father played a significant role as well. My dad would say that it was God's will, and that may be true. It doesn't hurt to acknowledge a few people along the way though. For them I was eternally grateful.

For my mom, I had just bitterness and judgement for appearing to give up and continue her drinking. While others fought, she drank. What small glimmer of forgiveness I briefly considered after the passing of Alison's mom, was destroyed.

***

Shortly after my dad's fight with cancer, my parents moved further away, to a town called Grand Coulee.

While my parents seemed to be isolating geographically, I did so emotionally. I focused a lot on my marriage, my career and myself. Phone call frequency to my parents was cut significantly. When I did call, it was not unusual to hear my mom trying to butt in on conversations while drunk, while dad would get agitated and tell her to, "shut up, I'm on the phone." If I spoke to my mom, it was for Mother's Day or her birthday. Not only did it just anger me to hear her speaking to me drunk, she was obnoxious. To hear her repeat herself three or four times within a conversation was not unusual. I would start thinking of excuses to get off the phone the moment I dialed, it was exhausting.

For the first few years, Alison tried to coach me through the relationship. She would encourage me to be patient, understanding and forgiving. At first, I was tolerant. Before long however, I started getting agitated.

Alison would say things like, "Only your mom can make the choice to change, being angry with her does nothing. All you accomplish is anger."

I finally arrived at a point where I was done hearing how I needed to get over myself. I finally said, "You didn't grow up with an alcoholic, I did. Stop telling me how wrong I am. She makes the choice to drink. She makes the choice to be a lousy parent. She makes the choice to drink while my dad is fighting for his life. She always makes the choice to put alcohol first."

Alison stopped trying to help my relationship with my mom. Finally, I was able to live my life blissfully with my head in the sand. Forgetting that she existed except on special occasions. Isolating myself just became easier. Everyone else seemed to be excusing or accepting of her addiction, I couldn't handle it. My dad even said one day on the phone, "You know, your mom has really mellowed out on her drinking."

My response?

"Wow dad, that's great. I'll believe it when I see it though."

As time went on, my parents, specifically my dad, stopped being forthright with me about issues they were having. Specifically, my parents stopped telling me about medical issues. Often, I was the last to know and often got news from my little brother.

It hurt. It cut. Deep.

I brought it on myself.

Then, I slowed down the flow of information that I gave out. At first, just to my parents, then the behavior eventually trickled down to my wife. Alison and I were best of friends for many years. We made each other very happy. We shared some very low lows and many amazing positive experiences. As I walked myself further down the path of isolation though, our bonds strained. More and more of our off time was spent apart, even vacations. Once Alison took a shift work job that caused us to work different shifts, the end was inevitable. The fault was not hers, I was alone a lot. I thought about kids. I thought a lot about the decision I'd made to live my life without them.

I was torn.

I debated with myself, was it kids I wanted or just more attention? If I wanted attention, then why didn't I work harder for it? Why did I force myself away from everybody? Why didn't I jump through hoops and make sacrifices to make sure we worked similar hours? I was very confused.

I sunk into deep depression. I didn't understand depression, so I didn't know how to deal with it. I saw my doctor about it, her answer was to fill me up with anti-depressants. The drugs didn't work and frankly had side effects that only seemed to compound my problems. I considered turning to the bottle which only made me think about my mom. I got angry with myself for even considering it, I wouldn't let alcohol take over my life like it had mom's.

Prescription drugs weren't the answer.

I wouldn't allow alcohol to be an option.

It felt like I had nobody to turn to. Nobody to talk to who could understand. I was alone. Isolated.

I wanted to just run away. I wanted to not care about jobs, car payments or mortgages. I wanted to leave family and friends behind, just start over. I talked to Alison about it. I shared with her my desires for the two of us to start over somewhere else. Even if it meant job transfers and not a true restart, I just wanted change. I wanted to control *something*.

Alison didn't want to move anywhere.

I felt stuck, in emotional purgatory.

***

Early in 2012 I was sitting on the master bedroom floor, next to me sat a loaded pistol. I was weighing the pros and cons of taking my life. Who would miss me? I felt all alone in the world. I wondered if it would hurt. I didn't want Alison to find me like that, should I call the police first and leave the door unlocked? Alison would think she had failed me, how could I do it in a way that she would understand? Alison was a loving wife who only ever treated me with respect and dignity, how I felt had nothing to do with my marriage. I simply felt alone. I didn't know how to make myself happier. What had a life of anger done for me? Alison could find a better man I thought. Maybe it would be better if I drove somewhere away from home and let strangers find me.

I felt lost in my identity. I had lost who I was.

As I sat there, my mind racing from option to option and weighing the consequences for those left behind, I felt something touch my arm. My Boston Terrier, Joey. My little puppy rescue had walked up while my eyes were closed in reflection and was licking my arm.

I couldn't do it.

One life on Earth depended on me, Joey. My little Boston Terrier with the Elvis smile saved my life. The precious soul I had pulled out of an animal shelter wasn't the rescue, he did the rescuing. I would just have to work on my issues, for him.

Chapter 20

Summer of 2012, I was sent to Madison Wisconsin for union training. While sitting down for dinner at the hotel restaurant, a woman sat down a few seats away and struck up a conversation with me. Her name was Britney. During the conversation, we talked about many things. We talked about children the most. We exchanged contact information. For the remainder of my stay in Madison and travel home, I was very introspective.

How many dreams had I allowed to go unrealized because of; other people, fear of change or fear of failure? Living my dream as a fighter pilot was never going to happen, but I *was* still able to have kids and mold a family in the image I envisioned.

I found myself at a crossroads.

I could stay with Alison. I could remain loyal to a woman who had never mistreated me. I could keep the beautiful house on the East side of Lake Washington and see my wife in passing until the day that we were each established in our careers enough to dictate schedules. I could plan a yearly vacation where just she and I went away while the rest of the year was spent in isolation.

Or.

I could risk all. I could take a chance with a woman like Britney to see what kind of father and family man I could be.

I could try my hand at being a sole provider and live a bit more modestly.

There was no promise of happiness in either choice.

There was no promise that either choice would work out.

All I knew was, something was missing from my life. I wasn't sure it was children, I thought it might have been. I felt that my dishonesty about not needing to have children in my life was coming back to kick my ass.

Late August 2012 I made my decision. I thought my long-term happiness would be better served if I moved on from Alison. I knew it would be possible to live the rest of my life with Alison, and I would always be respected and loved. However, I didn't think I could live the rest of my life without trying to have children of my own. So, I sat down with Alison and told her I wanted to leave. I told her that while I thought everything would be ok without children when we decided to marry, I found myself now desiring the opportunity.

That conversation was the most difficult of my life.

Alison was remarkably composed during the conversation. Emotional? For sure, yet very composed. We talked about options like counseling, though I told her I doubted going that route would yield results that would keep us together.

My mind was made up.

***

On the final day of August 2012, I moved into a small one-bedroom place in Tacoma. I finally told my parents what had transpired and where I had found a place. That's just how I had come to communicate with my parents during that time period. Generally, they got information from me well after I'd made decisions. Word got to them as a courtesy. I seldom called anymore for advice. Both of my parents were very upset for me. My dad seemed amazed that I had left the house Alison and I had purchased, while my mom kept saying how much she liked Alison. When I told them why I had made my decision, they seemed cautiously optimistic.

A few days later Britney flew in. She was all about kids. Britney, in fact, already had two children who were living with their dad. When I asked her why she didn't have custody of her kids, I was told "Because my ex-husband's attorney told lies about me and I could not afford my own". She also told me things like "He used to hit me" and "He's unstable and bi-polar".

Within about a month of dating I began to notice that liquor I kept on hand was going missing without me ever opening them. When I asked Britney about the missing liquor she would say, "I just made a drink". *With a whole bottle of liquor?!*

Frankly, I wanted to *believe* she was a good person. I wanted to believe that I had ended my marriage with Alison for a good reason. I wanted to believe that issues springing up in our first few months were small, just a symptom of changing scenery for Britney. Liquor consumption on the scales I observed were temporary because of stress from separation over children. I wanted to believe that if I could help her get increased access to her existing children and if we were to have children, she would mellow out.

So I turned a blind eye to her alcohol abuse.

Other issues that arose in the first months together with Britney, were her outrageous insecurities. There are countless instances I could point to in illustrating illogical insecurity on destructive levels, but I will limit them to two.

First, I have always kept photo albums from my youth and early adulthood. In my first album, there were two pages of high school graduation. Among the photos on those pages were pictures of a very close high school friend and me embracing. We were close, the photos were completely reasonable and in good taste, yet they concerned Britney. When I asked why, she became very defensive and said I either part with the pictures or her. I reluctantly shrugged my shoulders and allowed Britney to throw out those pictures along with others she found in a keepsake box of the same friend.

The second example had to do with my account on Facebook. One of my fellow Marines had her profile picture set to one where she was wearing a bikini on a California beach. Now, I had not commented about it, nor had I ever talked about her. Still, once Britney saw that picture, apparently as she scrolled through my friends, in her mind that woman became a threat. The idea was beyond stupid. Britney insisted that I "unfriend" the woman or risk losing her. Whatever, it was social media so I did. In my mind, it was not as if doing so made that Marine less of a friend. The pattern was beginning to wear on me though. I tried explaining to her, "Look, do you have any idea the quality of person I ACTUALLY walked away from? These other women are of no romantic interest to me, if I had wanted to do something about that, it would have happened long ago." The logic did not register with Britney, her insecurity was becoming a real problem, yet I enabled her and stayed.

By the end of 2012 I had finalized the divorce with Alison and remarried. I married Britney without my parents actually meeting her face to face.

In the early months of 2013 we began trying to conceive a child. By the end of February Britney was pregnant. I was so incredibly thrilled. Even in the early weeks before much development had even happened, I read every night to the little bump and even sang some songs. Every moment that passed I focused on how to make the pregnancy a success and researched things I could do for the baby and Britney. I shopped for healthier foods and kept snacks on hand that would mitigate nausea. We even brainstormed names for boys and girls in the early weeks. I called my parents with the happy news. Dad and mom were both happy for me, and even talking to my mom while she was clearly drunk was not as intolerable. In those early weeks of pregnancy I truly felt that I had made all the right decisions. I was ready to be super dad.

Shortly after the call to my parents, I caught Britney drinking. I was furious. The argument that ensued was epic. In my mind there was no excuse to risk the health of our young fetus for any reason, especially alcohol. I told her she was selfish. I told her the decision to drink was moronic. I told her she was sabotaging our future. I told her we needed to get to a doctor at the earliest possible time. All of those things were said at the highest volume I dared without risking a neighbor calling police.

Britney floored me. She said, "Alcohol in smaller quantities is no risk to the baby. I'm not going to see a doctor this early. You yelling at me is only going to hurt the baby. We're better off if you just accept it and leave me alone."

Utter disbelief.

I left her alone.

Days later she miscarried.

It was on that day and subsequent weeks that I understood an entirely new level of resentment and hatred for alcoholism. That woman, who I had risked so much for, elected to haphazardly risk the life of an unborn child simply for the choice to feel a good buzz. I wondered if my mom had imbibed during her pregnancies. I felt hopelessly trapped. Part of me wanted to get rid of Britney right then and see if Alison would want to reconcile. I desperately wanted out. I could not do that though. Even broaching the idea with Alison would have been grossly unfair to her emotional health. Additionally, I knew that I could not go back for myself.

I talked to nobody about all of my inner turmoil at that time. Years before I might have called my dad. What would he say in that moment to me? *I'm sorry for your loss*? *Stick it out*? *If you love her then you'll forgive*? That last thought would bring me to instant anger. Nobody understood. What should they really tell me I thought. *You made this decision, you stick with it. You agreed to marry an alcoholic, what did you expect dummy. Grass isn't always greener, I told you so.*

Except, nobody told me so. Nobody had the knowledge or guts to tell me I was a damn fool. I guess to anyone watching casually from the sidelines, Britney was just some midlife crisis I would have to work through.

About a month after the miscarriage, Britney asked if I would consider transferring to her home state of Minnesota so that she could get closer to family, especially her kids. Talking me into the transfer was not a tough sell. I wanted out of there badly anyway. The traffic and cost of living were shortening my life with each passing day. Though, I had not envisioned Minnesota. Britney sold it like this; "There's more opportunities for me to stay busy and work there. I'll probably even drink less."

So, I thought on it for an hour or two and then assured her I would see if any openings were available for me to transfer into. Turned out, a facility only about an hour from her hometown had openings. I didn't discuss the decision with anybody, rather I just applied that day. A few weeks later I was notified of my approved move to Rochester, Minnesota.

As Britney and I set out to getting ready for a move, I noticed a lot of my stuff started disappearing. Yearbooks, autographed baseballs, clothing, saved military correspondence from home, and much more all began turning up missing. When I questioned Britney about the missing items, she admitted to disposing of most of it and selling a few things. I was able to salvage my senior yearbook on the day she tossed it, but all else was lost or sold. Britney even urged me strongly to re-home my dog,

Joey. I told her that suggesting I do so was a definitive line in the sand. I told her, "Joey saved my life, you didn't. I will re-home you before I ever consider doing that to him."

About a month before the scheduled move my brother and his wife hosted a party at their house to send us off. My parents were there along with my brother's family. Britney insisted on having something to drink there, so she had me buy her a large bottle of wine. My mom may have had a glass out of the bottle, but Britney drank the majority of that bottle herself. Mom stuck to beer for the most part that night. I just remember thinking that night; *damn these two women cannot survive even basic family social functions without soaking their bodies in booze.* A whole bottle of wine? That's not casual consumption, it's a problem, especially when you're the only one getting that drunk. I was truly sickened to see my new wife behaving so similarly to my mom. What had I done?

***

By Mid-August of 2013 Britney and I had arrived in Minnesota. We had to stay with her dad and stepmom for a few days while the house we had rented was vacated. I had spoken on the phone with my new in-laws, but this was my first time meeting them face to face. Britney insisted I call them "mom" and "dad" which made me very uncomfortable since I hardly knew them, I felt they had not earned that level of endearment yet. However, I placated her and did as she asked. They seemed as unnerved by it as I did.

Britney's dad attended AA meetings twice a week and had been sober for some time. During those few weeks staying with my new in-laws, I gained a fresh perspective and insight into Britney through her parents. Her dad was especially candid with me. He told me that Britney needed to get into AA. He told me that Britney often called him drunk while I was at work. He told me that she had been an alcoholic for years and her addiction was one of the primary reasons Britney was so restricted in seeing her kids. The ex-husband was not a narcissistic control freak, he was just protecting his kids. Britney's dad seemed to pity me.

I said to him, "Well maybe if I can help Britney get regular contact with her kids, she wouldn't feel the need to drink so heavily."

He scoffed and said, "Ok, good luck."

I ended up renting a house in Preston, Minnesota. Preston is a quiet little town in Southeast Minnesota, about 40 minutes South of Rochester. The house was very old, over 100 years. Two stories with two bedrooms upstairs, with a small nursery off the master which was not heated. Another unheated bedroom downstairs off a small dining area and carpet throughout (including the kitchen.) There was a small shed outside attached to the house via a dog run and a detached garage with no insulation. My new block was very quiet, only three houses on each side of the street. Three of my five new neighbors were very pleasant and outgoing. One of my neighbors even mowed all my grass through the end of summer just to save me the trouble of buying a new lawn mower right away.

By October 2013 the temperatures really started to drop in Minnesota. I first remember freezing temps and snow toward the end of October or early November. When the snow came, it stayed. Once the mercury hit freezing, we would not see a thaw until the following spring. I thought I knew cold miserable weather, I did not. That first winter in Minnesota was among the most brutal in recent memory among my new Minnesotan friends at work and neighbors. At one point between December '13 and February '14 a record was set for the most consecutive days below zero in that area. I in fact remember one week where there were two days with wind chills in the negative 40's. The cold was so brutal, that winter I went through two car batteries on the same car.

After the move, Britney also tried to persuade me to talk to my brother less. Why she had misgivings about my family, she would not say. In that case I told her, "You can go straight to fuck off. I love my brother, and he'll be there for me long after you decide to leave."

Also in that winter, Britney became pregnant again. The miscarriage that took place back in Washington was still fresh in my memory, I wanted to be excited, but I was scared for the child. I knew Britney was drinking. There was nothing I could do to stop her. I did not know how severely she was drinking because she hit the bottles hardest while I was working nights. I would frequently come home to her sleeping, so my exposure was primarily in the mornings and early afternoons before work and through email. So, in a sense I was shielded from reality, but I knew there was an issue.

I plead with Britney.

I said, "Please, it would mean everything to me if you can find a way to be sober for this pregnancy. All I want is for the two of us to have a beautiful healthy baby, all I'm asking for is for you to put this pregnancy above your alcohol for 9 months."

Britney looked at me in such a contemptuous way and said, "I don't drink enough to affect the baby. Don't put that on me. You just do what you can and leave me alone about it."

I hated her for that.

It would only be a matter of time I knew, this one would fail too.

This time would be different. This time I would not allow myself to become attached until I had to, third trimester maybe. This time I would not allow myself to be let down, to be hurt.

I felt like I had made a big mistake. This woman was clearly wrong for me, yet I felt compelled to see things through. I felt like I had sacrificed so much and been so stubborn in my convictions, I HAD to try and MAKE this work.

Deep down I wanted her out of my life. I just didn't know how.

Weeks after the positive pregnancy test I received an urgent call at work from Britney, she was crying and drunk. I asked her what was wrong.

Britney, "Just get home, I wrecked your car pretty bad."

I was pissed. "How did you wreck my car?!"

Britney, "You need to get home, I think I'm losing the baby. I tried to go to a clinic and tore up the side of the car backing out of the driveway. Get home fast, I need to get to an ER."

I'm not sure she could have constructed any sequence of words to maximize my anger more than that. Not only had she been reckless with her body and the pregnancy, she had tried to drive my car drunk and emotional. If she hadn't torn up the car trying to back out of a driveway, who knows how many people she might have hurt in that reckless mindset along the way. I convinced my boss to let me leave work.

Upon arriving at the house forty minutes later, I observed what I had expected to find. The aftermath of a second failed pregnancy in the toilet, and a completely wasted blubbering drunk sitting there crying.

There was nothing that could have been done. Whatever had caused two miscarriages in one year, I cannot be certain. What I was certain of was how little Britney seemed to care in relativity to her addiction. Nothing could stop her from drinking. I was angry of course, but far more emotionally detached. My silence might have scared her a little. I didn't yell or vent at all. Rather, I quietly stewed. Britney pried for a response, I just shrugged my shoulders and told her I wasn't surprised. I told her that it was hard to get excited or attached when I saw how she was treating her body. I told her I didn't imagine a high concentration of vodka was good for a fetus. I told her we obviously had different priorities.

***

A few months after the miscarriage, winter finally ended and spring came. I sat down with Britney and told her that I felt we needed to take a break from trying to have kids and focus on our marriage. Further, I told her that it was time for her to get a part time job to help out. She didn't like anything I had to say, especially the part about working.

I took a lesson from my childhood. When my dad came to grips with a lack of control over mom's addiction, he told her to drink all she wants so long as she works and pays for it. So I told Britney, "Look it's obvious you really just care about vodka. Drink all the vodka you want, but you pay for it."

Within a few weeks Britney had a job on some farm a few towns over where she would apparently be paid cash on a daily basis. Yet, she continued to drink on my dime. I opened a new account at the bank with only my name on it, moved my direct deposit over and waited. Within a day she confronted me about cutting her off. I told Britney that it was no longer an option to drink away so much money that I had to struggle for rent and utilities. I told her again, if you want to drink, earn your own money and pay for it.

Days later I came home from work one morning and she was gone. During the night she had simply just vanished. No emails, no texts, no voicemails and no note. Just gone.

I called and texted to no end, but for silence.

In a way I was happy, yet I had to be sure she wasn't rolled over in a ditch somewhere dying without being reported missing. That would not have looked good on me.

So, after having been up all night at work, I drove the roads between Preston and this farm she allegedly worked at looking for her in ditches. Nothing.

Finally, I spotted her vehicle at the farmer's house, and I knew. Britney's cash flow had been cut off, she needed a new guy to exploit who would feed her addiction. I left her there.

That day, without sleep, I went to the hardware store and changed all the locks. Next I moved all of the stuff she owned and left behind out onto the all-season porch so that if Britney wanted it, she need not enter the house. When that was done, I called sick into work. I stayed up all of the next night figuring out what I needed to do. Do I look for a transfer back to Washington?

On day two of Britney's absence I called my dad, mom answered. She asked how I was doing, I told it all. Mom cried and begged me to come back to Washington, she wanted me to get a job at Grand Coulee Dam nearby my parent's home. I told mom it was unlikely I'd move back to Washington and if I did it wouldn't be Grand Coulee. Then I asked to speak to my dad.

My dad came on the phone with a voice and tone that sounded so sweet, and for the first time in over a day I allowed my guard to come down and I cried. I told him what had happened just as I had told my mom. I told him I hadn't slept in nearly two days. I asked him if he knew Britney was an alcoholic, and he quietly said, "Yes son."

Then I asked my dad, "How did this happen? How did I marry someone just like mom?"

Dad sighed, "I don't know son. What will you do now?"

I had no idea where my life was headed, all I knew was I wasn't going to go backwards.

A few moments passed and my dad asked, "Will you try and get Britney back?"

Having her back in my life was the last thing I wanted, yet I felt compelled to ask my dad if it was worth trying.

Frustratingly my dad answered my question with one of his own, "I don't know son. Do you love her?"

NO! *I loved the idea of what she could have been.*

Instead I answered, "I don't think so dad. I don't think I want her back in my life."

Dad and I chatted for a bit longer, he told me to sleep. He told me to call him back the next day. He told me to get back to work so that I wouldn't just sit in a house all alone.

I didn't listen, I called in sick for a second day.

That night I cleaned. I wanted that area, that house purified of Britney. I didn't want any trace of her in my presence. While cleaning I found thirteen empty vodka bottles behind the dishwasher. Several other vodka bottles were found elsewhere throughout the house, some hidden lazily, other stashes were clever. All reminded me of childhood. I thought, *this behavior is so familiar, how did I ever put up with it by choice?*

What that cleanse did for my emotional health was empower me with resolution. Where in the conversation with my parents I was pretty sure there was no taking Britney back; exposing the extent of her cover up attempts and filling a lawn sack with vodka bottles gave me absolute clarity. There would be no reconciliation.

Going into a third day without sleep I considered making a trip to the liquor store nearby for a small bottle of whiskey to help my mind settle. As I was getting dressed, the hypocrisy hit me in the face. *If I use alcohol to cope with my problems, how am I any different from mom or Britney?*

Instead I sat in quiet reflection and made a pact with myself. It goes like this:

I will never drink alcohol when I'm sad.
I will never drink alcohol to deal with a problem.
I will never drink alcohol around kids.
I will never drink alcohol on days or eaves I work.

So there I sat, just Joey and me. Day three of no sleep had begun. I sat in a chair with that little pup, Joey snoring by my side and put on a boring show. Finally, on the third day my brain rested and I slept.

Chapter 21

Once I was finally able to sleep things started getting better for me. For starters I went back to work. At work I was able to reintegrate with people and focus on something besides starting my life over. I arranged for counseling. Counseling helped me out tremendously. Where I had denied myself the opportunity to mourn my failed relationship with Alison before, counseling had set that to right. I was able to reflect through the help of a professional on all the things that made me happy. I was able to learn more about myself and why I behaved in certain ways.

For example I didn't know that I was an introvert. Until then I had just thought I was a loner and highly anti-social. I wasn't anti-social, I just functioned better in small groups for small periods of time and usually best in groups of people who valued one on one interactions. I did not function well in large groups with little intimate contact, the types who only exist on superficial planes.

Another crucial concept I took from counseling was that I functioned poorly in making other people happy because I wasn't focusing on what made me happy. I was able to make personal sacrifices to the point of allowing myself to become depressed so long as the sacrifice functioned to appease the other person. For example: if Britney felt insecure and threatened by the existence of photos where I was embracing a female friend, rather than stick up for myself, I would allow her to dispose of the pictures.

As a result of counseling I sought to make my wrongs right. I started by contacting the female friend I had cut contact with and apologized for allowing Britney to drive a wedge between us. She of course forgave me and helped me get back on my feet emotionally in the following weeks. It was as if she was just sitting there waiting to pick up the pieces.

I messaged the female friend who Britney made me "unfriend" over a bikini profile picture and apologized. I told her that I was proud to have that fellow Marine as a friend and I was ashamed to have let someone tell me otherwise. That particular friend had not known what had happened, she just laughed. She said, "Unfriending on Facebook did not make our friendship disappear. What a dumb bitch, of course I forgive you."

So it went. I slowly set my life back to normal equilibrium. I started watching movies and shows again that had females in it, Britney had been controlling of that since attractive females on screens were apparently a threat to her. Essentially all she would have on were animation and old 1980's sitcoms. I got back into my passion for gaming. Then I reestablished myself on Facebook.

Britney had taken it upon herself to shut down my Facebook account in 2013. She had felt that I had too many female friends there. When I had asked her which in particular were threatening to her, the one person she picked out was one of my cousins. I shook my head at the time and told her I didn't care one way or the other. Now that she was gone, it was time to reconnect with the world.

In the summer of 2014 I was sitting in my living room casually doing a scroll through the Facebook newsfeed. I happened upon a post by a woman who I had gone to middle school and high school with, Shannon Lloyd. In the post she had said, "Single parent issues. When a co-worker asks why I have to get home and mow my own grass, it's because that's what single parents do."

Shannon and I had talked once by phone since graduation. The phone call took place back in 2011 and I had discussed with her where I was in life. I remember the conversation from my end being in reference to being restless and wanting more. On that particular day Shannon was talking to me from a football field in Oklahoma, watching her daughter do a pom routine. I did not even take from the conversation in 2011 her relationship status. I must have just assumed that since she had young children, Shannon must be married.

Since I assumed Shannon was married, it stuck out to me when she posted about mowing her own yard as a single parent and I made a comment on the post. *I thought you were married?*

From that post sprung a flurry of texts and phone calls in the subsequent days. Shannon herself had been divorced a couple of times. Shannon had her life in order. She was autonomous with her own job and benefits, wasn't a drinker, and had two young kids and most importantly showed interest in me as I was. I didn't have to fake anything. I told her upfront everything I had been through over the past few years. I told her it felt like I'd allowed another person to restrict my true self and wasn't going to let that happen again. I told Shannon that I wouldn't let anyone tell me who my friends were, restrict access to them or try to separate me from family and my dog. I told Shannon that at one point I had seriously considered taking my own life over hopelessness and depression and that now was the time to make myself happy. I told her I had learned that if I can't make myself happy, then there was no chance I could bring happiness to anyone else. I told her that alcoholism would be a deal breaker. I essentially put it all out there. Early chemistry between Shannon and me was very good, still I was a little scared that she might have thought I was being too assertive in putting my welfare first.

The exact opposite effect was true.

I truly feel that Shannon appreciated that I had taken charge of my life and the direction I was going. I think that she found my honesty and candid conversation refreshing. I believe she felt as though she could be authentic with me since I was putting it out there who the real Matt was.

In retrospect it seems to me that the primary reason Shannon and I found chemistry so fast was our honesty with each other. I truly feel that if I had played the cautious game where little information of any importance was withheld for months, she would have smelled something rotten and avoided me altogether.

Shannon Lloyd didn't need me. That fact is what made her so incredibly attractive to me. If she had been some damsel in distress that had to have me around just to function, I might have kept things at friend levels. She didn't need me. She wanted to see if having me in the lives of her and the kids would uplift them in positive ways.

That was what made Shannon so intriguing to me.

I called my old friend from high school and told her about my conversations with Shannon and asked what she thought.

She said, "Matt, you're going to marry that girl. She is exactly what you need."

***

Once Shannon and I reconnected, our lives launched into an all-new and exciting direction. If I wasn't at work, I would be home with my laptop opened to Skype. We would video chat for hours, just soaking up all the information we could about each other. So often was my laptop on Skype, the internet service provider started sending me big bills for going way over my data limits. So, I setup a business account where I paid a bit more on a flat rate for unlimited usage.

Everything seemed so perfect, yet after two failed marriages I really wanted to protect myself and cover all bases with Shannon. I told her I could not sacrifice certain things anymore and I laid them out.

For one, it had to be ok for me to be myself. I have a passion for video games, and I told her so. It is how I prefer to relieve stress. Some people smoke, others drink, I choose to kill pixels through video games. It calms me and makes me happy. With that out there I also told Shannon, "Look I love video games and I will not give it up, but I will also not put that before family."

I told Shannon that my little pup, Joey, and I are a package deal. I would not be happy in the long term with a person who could not see the value or passion in the relationship I shared with my little rescue. I truly felt that I was still alive because of him.

I shared with Shannon that my friends and family are important and I couldn't be happy with someone who wanted to isolate me from them.

To put all of those concerns and others out there is scary if you think someone is special to you. It takes a certain courage to be willing to walk away from someone if they cannot respect your values and priorities. That courage is important though. When you've been unsuccessful in two marriages, one of the most important lessons you learn is: identify those things in a partner that you will not tolerate. I made this lesson into an exercise after Britney. I sat down and wrote out all the things in a partner I would immediately walk away from. I also wrote down a profile for the type of person who I thought would make me happy. Shannon fit my profile to near perfection, only one thing on my ideal profile didn't match Shannon, she couldn't have kids.

Shannon had to undergo a kidney transplant while we were still in high school. A side effect of the several surgeries she had to endure was that she couldn't get pregnant. Even if she were able to, the combination of medications taken post-transplant and other factors made the prospect of bearing a child through delivery very risky to the baby and herself. Delivering would be too taxing on her, so much so that it could kill her. Since she was unable to procreate, Shannon and her second husband elected to adopt children instead. A boy and a girl who were biologically brother and sister, born barely more than a year apart, were 6 and 7 years old respectively when we reconnected.

Potential children aside, Shannon, appeared ideal in every other way I had conceived. She had a good job, so she didn't need me to support her. Shannon was fiercely independent and strong intellectually. She had shown exceptional resilience and character through organ transplants and failed marriages. I could not think of a single person who had shown me such unfiltered honesty and integrity. Lastly, she was not an alcoholic.

There was only one decision to make, was I ready to concede the idea of having children of my own?

***

To Shannon's credit, it was clear she wanted to have me in her life, yet she knew through our numerous conversations via Skype how important children were to me and she wanted to make sure I knew it would be ok if I wanted something else. Knowing that she was willing to say, "I want you in my life, but if you have to pursue someone who can give you kids, then so be it" was an incredible showing of courage and integrity on her part.

I had already promised my first wife that I was ok with not having kids. With Britney I had tried for a year and a half to force a family. Two miscarriages later, I had to admit my folly. Now, there was Shannon. An ideal person for me in every other way, so good a person I could not afford to be wrong again. I could not ruin the life of her and her two kids.

I reflected for weeks. I weighed how much I really wanted to go through conceiving children and everything that comes after. Finally I came to a painful realization, maybe I wasn't meant to father children. Maybe there was something else I was meant to do. Maybe Britney had miscarried twice for a reason. Divine intervention? I wasn't sure I bought in fully to the idea of God meddling in pregnancies. God or no, I had an epiphany of sorts. Why hadn't Shannon and I come together after high school? Why now? Why after twenty years had our paths collided?

I needed to be around her in person. I needed to get a feel for what family dynamics I could expect that are not apparent through phone calls and Skype. I scheduled a trip to visit Shannon in Oklahoma for November of 2014.

***

On November 2, 2014 I left Minnesota for Oklahoma. Winter was already upon Southern Minnesota and the heater had gone out in my Lincoln Navigator. I bundled Joey up in a sweater and blankets, loaded his doggie bed on the passenger seat and hit the road. As the temperatures outside slowly crawled up the further South I drove, so too did my anticipation. Whenever I tried to stop and rest along the way, I simply could not sleep. So much was on my mind. How would it feel if Shannon was disappointed in what she saw in person? How would her kids get along with a man in their mom's house? Would I even like Oklahoma?

About 14 hours after leaving Minnesota, I pulled into Shannon's driveway just outside of Oklahoma City. We embraced, we kissed, and we just looked at each other. Seeing someone everyday over Skype could not replace how it felt to be welcomed and accepted. Those first days together were amazing. Shannon and I just seemed to fit together, as if we had been that way all along. There was no need to be fake or pretend to be someone I wasn't.

Shannon had already seen the real me for months via Skype. I could be authentic.

A few days after my arrival, Shannon's kids arrived from their dad's house. Kennedy, age 7 and Sloan, 6. Quite remarkable are Kennedy and Sloan, intuitive and smart. They seemed to sense and react in a certain synergy. Those kids seemed to feed off the energy of how Shannon and I were together, they too seemed happy. Kennedy and Sloan *wanted* me there. Those kids weren't tolerating me, they were integrating me. A few days later was Shannon's birthday and she had to work. The kids were not in school that day (a weekend I think), so I took them to the store and got ingredients for them to make Shannon cupcakes and supplies to make homemade birthday cards. Nothing about our being together was awkward. They worked right along with me in making Shannon's birthday amazing and it just wasn't weird. Kennedy and Sloan were already accepting me and respecting me in a fatherly role.

That day my decision was made. What I could not see for myself, two little humans helped me to figure out. Being a father didn't mean pregnancies, deliveries and same last names. Any fool can conceive a child. Being a dad meant actions. Being a real dad meant interacting with young kids you love and showing them how to be a person who cares about others. Being a dad for me would mean showing these two young children what it meant to have healthy relationships. It would mean showing them how to respect each other and be kind to one another. For Kennedy, being a dad to her would mean identifying what a real man was and showing her how she should expect to be treated. Being a dad to Kennedy would mean being there for her, every single day. Being a dad for Sloan would mean teaching him integrity and accountability. Sloan would know what a father is by example and mutual respect. Being a dad to both of them would mean loving their mom and respecting her. It would mean that when we disagreed on anything, I would show her respect and good communication skills rather than yelling and driving away for hours. Most of all, being a dad would mean being there, sober.

A few days later my vacation was up and it was time to get back to Minnesota. As Shannon and I stood in the driveway, I told her I would be back. She said, "Make it fast."

I said, "I will."

I did.

Chapter 22

In my career, transfers are not always expedient. Luckily for me, a position opened up in Oklahoma in December for my job and it was only 30 minutes from where Shannon lived. I applied and was accepted by the middle of January 2015. I started selling or donating everything I could not move. A week after my move was approved, Shannon and I met in Kansas City, Missouri for a weekend and I loaded up her trunk with things I wouldn't need for a few months. We got some Kansas City Barbeque and had a nice weekend together. The next time I would see Shannon would be moving day.

When I got back to Minnesota, I was given my official transfer date. March 1, 2015. I was so excited to get the hell out of Minnesota. Not that there is anything wrong with Minnesota or the people I worked with. Actually, they were quite nice. I was just so excited to kick off the next chapter of my life. February seemed to be 45 days long that year. By the middle of the month, time seemed to be moving in slow motion. I requested to spend some vacation hours and leave a few weeks early, they granted it. The day they granted my request, I sped home, loaded up the car with the remainder of my belongings, loaded up Joey, turned my key into the landlord and hit the road.

I called Shannon a few minutes after leaving Preston and said, "Guess where I'm at?"

Anticipation thick in her voice, "Where?"

"On my way" I replied.

Shannon gasped and said, "Shut up are you serious?"

I went on to explain to her that I simply just asked to leave early, and they let me. She couldn't believe it. I was finally, after hundreds of hours on Skype and a few dozen hours of driving going to be permanently in Oklahoma. Maintaining the speed limit was difficult that day to say the least. I was encouraged to do so in the early stages though, thanks to icy roads and a little snow. By the time Joey and I were about an hour into Iowa, the temperatures started crawling up. By Missouri, the outside temps were above freezing, and when I hit the Kansas turnpike temperatures were safely above freezing. From there it was a cannonball run to my new home. To Shannon.

Joey and I pulled into the driveway in just under 14 hours. I easily beat my November time. Shannon said, "Welcome home."

And, for the first time in over two years, those words rang true.

***

In the first few weeks of Shannon and I being together, we found a bigger house to rent than she had been in. With the exception of a few hours of help with heavy lifting, I nearly single-handedly moved the both of us myself while Shannon was at work. A fresh start for the both of us you could say.

In one of my first acts as a father to the kids, I bought Sloan a new lofted bed. That little boy was so excited. As the younger of the two, it seemed to me that Kennedy often got newer things first and besides that he was in more desperate need of an upgrade.

A few weeks later, as spring approached, Shannon and I went out and bought a lawn mower. That day I reminded her of the post on Facebook that had reconnected us. "Single mom problems….gotta mow my own yard." I told her, "You will never again have to mow your own yard."

In April of 2015 my family was having a reunion / birthday party for my grandma. Having just moved, I didn't have a surplus of money for travel on short notice to Washington and back. Aunts, cousins and my parents all said, "Wish you could come, but we understand."

Shannon actually had some unused airline vouchers she'd earned through performance at work. Flights she was no doubt saving in hopes of flying home to visit her family and friends. She approached me and said, "Do you want me to use my vouchers to send you home?"

We'd only been together a few short months and it meant a lot to me that she was willing to use them in that way. Knowing, it surely meant a longer time before she could fly anywhere. Of course I wanted to go home and be with my family, I wanted to take her with. There wasn't enough for both of us to go and Shannon assured me that it was ok. My generous new girlfriend thought it would be good for me to see them. She said, "It's really ok, you can go. I'll have to stay for Kennedy and Sloan anyway. When we go back together, it will be as a family. Can you promise you'll get me back there to visit as a family?"

I told her I could and will. She booked the flight. The only person I told about the trip on the other end was my brother. Someone had to pick me up from the airport.

My flight into Seattle arrived late in the evening. John was there as promised and we hugged. By the time we reached his house it was after midnight. I just crashed out on his couch. When morning arrived my niece and nephew found me on the couch and hugged me. It was so good to see family again. It had been nearly two years since I had seen any of them. I asked my brother, "Have you told anyone I'm here?"

He said, "No brother, I've kept your secret." The reunion was being held in Colville, Washington and my brother lived in Arlington. For those not familiar with Washington state geography, those towns are on opposite sides of the state. My parent's house was near Grand Coulee, which lies roughly halfway between. John said, "Well we better hit the road, it's a long drive."

John made good time driving us to our parent's house, despite all the stops we made along the way. Late afternoon we arrived at my parent's house. I could hardly wait to see the look on my folk's faces. Without knocking I just walked in. They were not in immediate sight as we entered, so I walked into the kitchen. My mom was the first one to walk into the kitchen after me. The looks of drinking were on her face, but I still smiled and said, "Hi mom."

She smiled back at me and said, "Oh hi John, I'm so glad you're here."

Now, I'll grant my brother and I have many features that make us similar in nature, but we are not remotely close to being twins. I'm a little bigger and he has the better smile.

I replied, "Mom, it's Matt."

She covered her mouth, nodded and teared up a little. Then she said, "It really is Matt, oh my god what are you doing here?"

I just smiled and said, "Well there *is* a family reunion happening isn't there? Where *else* would I be?"

Moments later my dad walked down the hall and saw me. Dad was shocked as well. One moment he had no expression in particular, the next he was smiling from ear to ear. He said, "Matthew is that really you? Are you really here?"

As my eyes watered up I had to choke on my words to get them out, "Yeah dad I'm here. We have Shannon to thank for that."

That trip ended up being amazing for me in so many ways. Everybody was shocked to see me, for some people in my family, it had been a very long time since I'd seen them. Ultimately mom didn't make the trip to the actual reunion, apparently she couldn't get the time off. Everyone else was there though and I loved every minute of it.

One thought that frequently crosses my mind in my travels, especially since I tend to go far from family for long periods of time is: *who am I seeing today for the very last time?* I know it's a bit morbid, borderline cynical even. I guess my mind works this way to make the most of each visit and tell people that I love them every single time I see them. I make an effort for everyone I love to tell them so, rather than assuming they know how I feel. A lesson I first learned when a cousin I held dear, died by gunshot. A lesson further driven home when Alison's mom perished in a house fire. So when the times come for goodbyes, I often wonder if any given goodbye is the final goodbye. I'll hug someone with more heart and tell a person I love them.

Regarding that trip in particular, there was more than one person I would embrace for the very last time.

***

Mother's Day of 2015, Shannon was sitting next to me when I picked up my cell phone and called my mom. It was early evening in Oklahoma, so afternoon in Washington and my mom was already truly drunk. So obvious was her level of intoxication, just in her greeting.

I sighed, "Hi mom, happy Mother's Day."

Mom gushed, "Oh thank you John. How are you doing?"

"Mom, it's Matt." Already, I was getting agitated. Were our voices really so similar?

"Oh sorry Matthew. You and John sound so alike." I shook my head and wondered if my parents had caller ID. Arriving at the conclusion that it didn't matter, I moved on.

I started filling mom in on what my new family had been up to and how the kids were doing. Then she interrupted me to complain about her job, my dad and other people. So I quietly sat there next to Shannon listening to my mom complain and then repeat herself again, and again, and again.

After about ten minutes of listening to my mother stumble and stutter through the same stories three times, I began sighing and rolling my eyes. Exasperation clear on my face Shannon looked me in the eyes with compassion and empathy and mouthed the words, "She's your mother, she gave you life."

While I was able to appreciate Shannon's sentiment, I didn't want to hear it. No doubt, she had heard the entire story from me via Skype about the relationship between mom and me. From Shannon's perspective, I'm sure it was an attempt to lighten my mood. She could see how I became tense and my body language shifted from relaxed to stressed. Changes in my postures that were involuntary to be sure, made from years a reliving trauma of living with an alcoholic over 18 years of my life and countless strained phone conversations.

I said to my mom, "Mom, I have to ....."

Mom, "Gibberish gibberish gibberish ..... Your dad"

"MOM."

More drunken rambling

"MOM! I have to go make dinner. I love you, goodbye."

I didn't have to go make dinner. It could have just as easily been, "Mom, I'm driving through a tunnel..." and she would not have been the wiser. Any excuse would work with my mom because she didn't truly listen anyway. I could tell her things about my life until I was blue in the face or tell her once, the results were the same. Here I was trying to be a good son and wish my mom a happy Mother's Day, only to have my disdain and resentment renewed.

I've been told many times over by people closest to me how obviously I wear my emotions on the outside. When it came to my mom, this was very true. Talking to her or about her had always rankled me into foul moods, no matter how happy I was. That day was no different.

Shannon, "You need to be patient with your mom, she gave you birth."

Because of my feelings for Shannon, because our courtship was new and because this was her first real experience in watching me interact with my mom I exercised great restraint and patience. "Shannon, we grew up very differently. You grew up with two parents who got along reasonably well, an only child who could expect on most nights for your parents to both be mostly sober and involved in your life. That wasn't me. Do I love my mom? Yes. I just can't stand talking to her."

In a testament to Shannon's level of understanding people, especially people she loves, she tried to understand through empathy rather than tell me I was wrong and judge. "Matt, we need to find a way for you to be ok with your mom, before she's gone."

I just shook my head and let the discussion end.

***

On a beautiful summer evening, Shannon and I were set to meet some friends for dinner at a restaurant next to a lake in Northwest Oklahoma City, Lake Hefner. Locals from the area frequently run or walk their dogs around the lake, while others cram onto patios of the handful of restaurants to socialize and observe spectacular prairie sunsets over the lake. Standing a football field away from the spot our group would sit was an old lighthouse.

A few weeks prior I had purchased a diamond ring.

Earlier in the day one of Shannon's friends and I were texting back and forth. I sent him an image of the ring and told him I would be asking Shannon to marry me later that night out by the lake. Only he and I knew of my plan for the evening.

Ring in my pocket, Shannon and I arrived at the lake. Shannon's friend brought his new girlfriend and we found a spot on the patio's edge. Looking back on it now, I know it's silly, but I was nervous as hell. We had discussed marriage and long-term plans, so logically I knew the answer, yet the actual act of proposing to her still filled me with butterflies. Our companions ordered drinks, we all ordered and ate food, I had still not asked. Shannon's friend kept looking at me with a grin while doing this movement with his eyes toward Shannon. As if he were saying, *well get on with it!*

Slipping the ring from my pocket I held it in my sweaty palms. I wanted to make the moment organic and special, while she genuinely seemed to have no clue I had made a plan to propose on that night. She just kept on talking and talking, I didn't want to interrupt.

Finally, a natural pause in the conversation came and I slipped from my chair as if to pick something up. When Shannon glanced at me, there I was, one knee with diamond ring in hand.

Shannon, "I hate you."

She was smiling, and perhaps a little misty. Her friend was wide eyed with a huge smile, while nobody else seemed to even notice what was happening. Perfect.

"Will you marry me?" Only the three of us heard her answer as I slipped the ring on her finger.

***

Wedding plans moved quickly with my brand-new fiancée, we had essentially been planning for this time for months anyway so it was easy. Shannon and I arranged to be married at the lighthouse on the very same lake I proposed at. Getting a large entourage committed from out of state would have been very impractical and cost burdensome on many people, so we kept it to a small group of local friends. Only one person from out of state arranged to fly in on short notice, my old high school friend who predicted I would marry Shannon.

On July 26, 2015 Shannon and I were married. To our surprise, my new bride's friend who was there for the proposal showed up with a wheelbarrow full of alcoholic drinks, literally a wheelbarrow. While I found the gesture unique and frankly pretty awesome, I would not partake. My brand-new step daughter and son were best man and maid of honor. In accordance with my self-imposed rules on alcohol, I forced myself to keep alcohol free. Possibly one of the biggest tests of my convictions and priorities, was that day. Frankly, I thought the occasion warranted a celebratory drink. My friend who flew in even offered to drive us home. All I kept telling myself was: *Unlike my mom, family will be priority over alcohol. What message am I sending if I can't keep promises to myself? What will I tell my brand-new family, especially the children, if I pick and choose the best times to hold true to my commitments?*

Later on that hot July day, after everything had settled down, I sat down and called my parents. Mom answered the phone, drunk.

I said, "Hey mom, you and dad have a new daughter in law and new grandchildren!"

Mom was very excited and happy, she gushed on and on about how much she and dad loved Shannon. As my mother carried on for a bit, I decided to just let her gush. After all, mom and dad weren't there to be part of the day, what harm was there in hearing her talk for a bit? I took the drunk talk as long as I could before telling her I had to go.

***

One of the first big decisions Shannon and I were faced with was a career decision for her. For a few years she had been working for a vanity publisher who didn't always treat her well, but they did pay her well. In addition to a nice salary they also covered her healthcare at 100 percent. Nice benefits which are hard to leave behind. However, there was a sense that the company was beginning to falter and she wasn't happy with many aspects of the business. So, I sat down with my new bride and we discussed options. One of our favorite plans was for Shannon to become an entrepreneur. Specifically, her passion is in coaching people who want to write and become published.

Like most new entrepreneurs, there were early struggles. Some things we struggled with early were finding new clients and what exactly this new business would look like. What would the identity be? What would be the best way to find people who needed help? We learned in the first months that the type of work Shannon enjoyed most was actually hearing people's stories, validating their purpose (or why it was important to them) and walking them through the process of getting the words from mind to paper. Several clients benefitted from her wide knowledge base in publishing and would pay her for different parts of the process such as editing, formatting or cover design. Yet, her true love is and always has been hearing a story and getting it written.

Over the course of about a year and a half after Shannon founded her business, Creative Literary Consultants, she has helped many people get published. Some of those books had even become Amazon best sellers. We have both felt very fortunate for Shannon to be involved with helping people get their stories published.

In the late fall of 2016 I was rummaging through some storage totes in our attic when I came upon a container filled with Marine Corps uniforms and papers I had kept. Among the contents was an old shoe box filled with letters my dad had written to me while I was in the Corps. I pulled the shoe box out, carried it down the steps, and then into our living room where I dumped the letters on the floor and spread them out. Most of the envelopes were of the smaller variety, but a few were standard paper width sized. One of those larger envelopes stood out, it was very thick, and so I pulled the contents out.

What I found, or re-discovered I suppose, were two typed out documents. Each, a re-telling of two traumatic experiences my father had lived through in Vietnam. Flashing back to my youth I recalled how often I would ask my dad to share with me his experiences. I remembered being starved for information about this sliver of time in the life of my father. So mysterious at that age because he simply refused to share with me. I even remember going so far as asking him if he had killed anyone. A memory that I am now ashamed to admit. I can scarcely believe I even asked the question. Even as I write now, the memory brings tears to my eyes that I would ask my dad to relive that.

As most anyone would expect, especially a combat veteran, those memories are traumatic. Finding a way to say the words out loud must be extraordinarily difficult, for reasons I cannot understand, yet hope to be empathetic about. So, at some point during my enlistment, perhaps in the months I was nervous about possible deployments to Iraq, my dad had taken the time and typed out two specific experiences in stunning candidness and detail. Two horrifically traumatic moments that must have been weighing on him for decades. Two documents that I hold dear, not because of their contents, but because of what it took for him to share them with me.

So there I sat, cross-legged on the floor like a child, tears streaming from my eyes and Shannon asked me what was wrong. I shook my head and handed her the stories my father had written. After she had read them, we cried together. When I had composed myself, I told her why those stories were so special to me.

Shannon and I discussed the stories and what it must be like to carry trauma around in your mind for so many years. Who could my father and those like him commiserate with? Who among those closest to my dad could possibly understand what he was dealing with? Among my father's concerns was his afterlife, would he be allowed into heaven for what he had done in Vietnam? What turmoil my dad and veterans like him are subjected to, wounds really, wounds that don't bleed. Wounds that deep down, don't really heal. How can you convince someone that everything is ok when they are convinced the Lord will reject them?

Before that day, Shannon had been contemplating ways for using the platform of her business to expand in philanthropic ways. On the day we cried over my dad's stories, an idea was born. Everyone knows the numbers, every day, 22 veterans take their lives. What if, we put together an organization whose sole purpose was to provide a means to help veterans achieve some peace through writing their stories down? What if, through writing their stories down, published or burned, they are able to give purpose to their pain and find some measure of healing? What if, those who are willing to share their stories were compiled into a book, say 22 chapters, each representing the 22 who take their lives and we publish the book? What if, proceeds from the books are funneled back to the next group of vets to cover costs of making future books and more veterans are helped? What if, we actually saved ONE life in an endeavor such as this?

On that day, with twenty-year old letters sitting on the floor and Shannon and I sharing tears over my father's stories, Books by Vets was born.

Within days of the genesis of Books by Vets, I called my dad. I shared with my dad the vision Shannon and I had regarding giving back to veterans. After chatting for a few minutes about how our plan to help veterans would work, I asked for his consent to include one of his stories in the book. At first, dad seemed a little wary, but after a little talking I convinced him. I can only guess about his reason for caution, though I would imagine that in part, it's difficult to make yourself transparent to the world. Shannon and I were very happy he consented because my father is exactly the type of people we wanted to help. We desired more with every grateful veteran who spoke to us, to find those who may have considered taking their lives over those invisible wounds.

***

February 4, 2017 I called my mom for her annual birthday phone call. Unlike most phone calls, I happened to catch her in a moment where she'd had little to no alcohol. What followed was a very pleasant conversation. Mom and I talked about the book Shannon was working on with dad's chapter. We talked about our kids. Mom wanted to write down on her calendar when the birthdays were for Kennedy and Sloan. Mom and I talked a little about my work and of course she complained a little about hers. She filled me in on dad's health status and we shared concerns about that. Dad had gone through some serious medical issues and I was especially keen on getting my opinion in her ear for what needed to be done to take care of him on a day she would actually hear me.

After about twenty or thirty minutes I decided it was time to end the call. "Hey mom, I have to go. Please make sure dad gets those issues checked out."

She said, "Oh I will son, we'll make sure of it. I love you."

"I love you too mom." End call.

**

It was not uncommon to go long stretches without getting calls from my parents. Mom knew the routine I think, she knew deep down I would quickly end calls when she called drunk. Additionally, dad was calling me more infrequently as well because he was having significant issues with hearing loss. Phone calls were very difficult for him.

Early morning phone calls are almost never good, they almost always mean something has gone very wrong. So, when my cell phone rattled on my nightstand at 3 AM on May 1st, 2017 and the caller ID said, 'Parents' my heart was jumping in my chest.

I answered the phone.

The voice on the other end was my dad, crying. "Matthew?"

"Yeah dad, I'm here. What's wrong?" I already knew.

"Matthew, your mom ...... your mom is gone Matthew." Sobbing. "Matthew, your mom has died, I have to go."

End call.

Part 3

"To forgive is to set a prisoner free and discover that the prisoner was you." - Louis B. Smedes

Chapter 23

With the abruptness of my father's call and its sudden end, I was left standing in our master bedroom, phone in hand, dumb struck.

Shannon asked me, "What's wrong? What's happened?"

I didn't cry. I set the phone down, looked at my wife and said, "My mom is dead."

Shouldn't I have been crying? Shouldn't I have been a sobbing mess in the arms of my wife? Why was I so devoid of emotion? Shannon looked shocked. Was it because my mom had died or was it because her husband appeared to be indifferent? She started to crack with tears and disbelief, "What?! Are you serious? Your mom?"

I slowly shook my head up and down at her and walked into the bathroom to look in the mirror. Where were the tears? What was wrong with me? I turned on the cold water spigot and washed my face. Shannon followed me into the bathroom and hugged me from behind. She said, "What can I do?"

This time I shook my head back and forth. I didn't know what to do, how could I tell her what needs to be done? I needed to get back to Washington, dad needed me. I started thinking about what I needed to do to get time off, arrange transportation and get a funeral planned. Furthermore, I wondered what kind of care my dad might need. What was his current status in terms of being able to take care of himself?

Once I got to thinking about my dad, a weird thing happened. I got angry with my mom all over again! In my mind I thought; *I can't believe you were so negligent to destroy yourself through alcohol until it killed you mom! I can't believe you left your husband all on his own in failing health! That man loved you, refused to leave you and how was his loyalty rewarded? Through sheer extreme alcoholic suicide.*

Look, even in the moment I knew my mind was not in a healthy place. I knew it. Shannon knew it. Everybody knew it. I pulled no punches for my disdain over my mom. I didn't want to hear about how wonderful she was. I had no desire to anoint her as a faultless angel in the afterlife either. Her death did not wipe out nearly 40 years of anger and resentment. Her death was not a relief nor was it a shock. I knew that the day would come, when a lifetime of alcohol abuse would take its due. You can't drink that heavily for that long without consequences. She had to know there would be consequences.

So, I didn't cry. I knew the day would come, it did for Papa. After all, my mother was her father's daughter.

As the sun rose over Oklahoma, I discussed with Shannon what I thought we needed to do. I would drive into work and secure a week off. Upon my return we would pack up the car and start out for Washington. It wasn't a particularly good plan, the plan left little time with family and lots of time on the road. Our problem was, at the moment we weren't prepared to drop over a thousand dollars on last minute airline tickets. Shannon touched base with her parents to let them know of our travel plans, they didn't like our plan any better than we did. In an act so selfless and generous, my mother in law purchased airline tickets for us along with a rental car.

Within 36 hours of the phone call from my dad, Shannon and I landed in Spokane, Washington. Shortly thereafter we were on the road headlong for Grand Coulee. I still had not cried.

I thought a lot about what I felt in those first 36 hours. Sure, I knew my anger and resentment issues ran ocean deep. Still, why wasn't I mourning the loss? What was Shannon thinking about her husband who wouldn't cry over the death of his own mother? Did she think I was some kind of robot? Actually, I started to concern myself more with making sure my wife knew I wasn't dead inside.

So we talked.

I told her exactly how I was feeling. What better way to fill a few hours of tough fatigued driving than legitimate thoughtful conversation?

Looking at my wife I offered, "Are you worried that I haven't cried?"

She looked back at me, thoughtful, "Well, I do find it a little odd. If the roles were reversed, I would probably be a complete mess. However, I know your feelings about your mom are complex, and I think you are just in mission mode. I believe you are just trying to find a way to make everyone ok, when you're ready the tears will come."

For a few moments I pondered her reply. There was a lot of truth and logic there. "Shannon, I'm mad at my mom. I'm mad at her for dying."

She appeared to weigh my words. "Why?"

Why? Why indeed. *Because she killed herself! Not with a pistol or anything fast, but with a gradual deliberate conviction that she needed fucking alcohol!!* "Sweetheart, I'm not exactly sure why. I think I'm conflicted. I knew this was coming, you'd have to be a fool to expect a long life for someone who abuses alcohol on those levels. I think I'm mad because my dad is all alone. I'm mad at her because her addiction seems selfish to me. I'm mad because there will be a service, and everyone there will paint this picture of a perfect spouse, mother, sister and aunt that just isn't authentic. I'm mad because for forty years of my life my mom has been a drunk and now everyone will just pretend that fact isn't so. I'm mad because having someone in the house could literally mean the difference of life and death to my dad. I'm scared shitless that we'll be back in a few months for my dad."

Shannon slowly nodded her head, as if she knew exactly what needed to be said, yet cautious that I may not be in a place to hear it. Finally after a few moments she responded, quietly, "Honey, you need to forgive your mom."

For the first time in my life, I actually thought about forgiveness. I just didn't know how.

***

Some people are just wired differently. While pulling into the driveway where an ambulance sat only a day prior, may be enough to unhinge some, for me I felt the need to assert control. I figured dad would likely be in shock and in some stage of the grieving process. Which stage I could not be sure. Expectations I had set for myself were; *a very real possibility exists that nothing has been done and I'll need to get straight to work.*

I had expected to make service arrangements, contact family, deal with funeral home people, run an obituary and who knows what else. I was relieved to find that dad was doing a little better than I had anticipated and the only major issue he had not addressed was a service. Shannon and I asked him what he needed, dad seemed to be in reasonably good shape as far as food and necessities. In truth, dad had done very well, he even arranged and paid for a hotel room for Shannon and me.

For the first time since his phone call, I was able to sit with my father and glean more details about mom's passing. She had collapsed, his attempts to revive her were proving unsuccessful and when first responders arrived, there was not much that could be done. Mom was beyond recovery methods the paramedics had. She never made it to the hospital. Cause of death, coronary failure.

Dad was actually beating himself up pretty bad for not being more effective with CPR. Clearly his stage of grief was, *I could have done more.*

No. No dad, you have done all you could for as long as you could. Alcoholism did this, not CPR skills. Mom's refusal to accept empirical evidence regarding what booze did to her body did this. All you've done for as long as I've been alive is try to persuade her to give up her stupid addiction. No. No dad you didn't do anything wrong, she did this to herself. "Dad, when it's time to go, it's time. There was nothing more you could have done. You did the exact right things, get first responders here as fast as possible. Please don't blame yourself."

By the look on my father's face I could tell he wasn't buying what I was saying, he just nodded his head in reflection. I wanted to scoop him up, wrap my arms around him and say, "It's all going to be ok." At that moment, I don't think he would have bought that either.

Slowly, over the course of hours family and friends poured into the house. First, my sister followed by my brother and his family. Shortly after my siblings, came my mother's siblings along with their spouses. Two of her sisters and one brother. Each time someone new arrived, my father was compelled to retell the events of mom's passing. Every single telling, the scab seemed to be ripped off for the fresh wounds to be revealed anew. The alpha dog protector in me wanted to put a stop to all of the morbid details. As if to say; *she's gone isn't that enough for you?* Yet, I could sense that with each telling he seemed a little stronger, and those who asked were receiving something they needed. So I instead sat quietly and observed.

One phrase that kept popping up was a classic, "Janet was her father's daughter." Which of course can be interpreted to mean; *Janet drank because her father drank. For Janet her booze wasn't a choice, it was a birthright.*

Every single time I heard those words I wanted to scream. What a load of bull!!! Janet drank because Janet liked to drink. It's not like she inherited blue eyes and gapped teeth! Such an enabling cop out that drove me to anger every single time I heard it. Holding my tongue that day took extreme restraint.

Early in the evening on the day of our arrival my father said, "Follow me son, I need to show you something." So I followed my dad as he walked outside and into his covered carport. At the carport entrance he stopped and gestured toward the far end from where we stood and said, "Look over there."

Looking toward the area dad gestured, stacked nearly to the carport ceiling or at least a few feet from it was a large mound of lawn bags, all filled with crushed beer cans. In that moment, for the first time in nearly two days, I had hope for my dad's long-term future. He wasn't in denial over the cause of mom's premature demise as I had feared. Rather, his reasoning was very practical. Dad said, "There son, your mom drank herself to death. All the warning signs were there to be seen, she just didn't want to quit."

In a tone that brokered not one inkling of righteousness, I quietly stated, "I know dad."

As evening befell Grand Coulee, the aunts and uncles slipped away to their hotel rooms. Meanwhile, I sat with my brother and sister and together we planned our mother's memorial service. For the first time that I recall in the history of being a big brother to those two, we all worked together and nobody fought or got their feelings hurt. We universally found agreement on how best to memorialize our mom, while dad sat nearby and relinquished control for the first time since she passed.

Janet Whittington, mom, would have been proud of her children.

Shannon and I arrived at our hotel room later that night. Considering the early hour we had to be through security in OKC, the day had been exceptionally long and exhausting. I sat on the bed and my wife asked how I was doing. Maybe she was looking for me to finally breakdown or perhaps Shannon was simply making sure I remembered that she was there for me. In truth, what I appreciated most about Shannon during that time was that she seemed to know I had to make sure business was handled. She knew I felt that showing weakness in front of my family wouldn't be an option. I felt like, at some point my leadership would be needed. Since I had to be tough, Shannon remained close by to be a safety net, ready for the moment I would fall apart.

We laid down to sleep after an incredibly long day around 10 PM. Dad had arranged a viewing for the next day, May 3rd.

I still had not cried.

***

After breakfast the following morning, Shannon and I met the immediate family at the funeral home for mom's viewing. I remember walking into the room where the funeral director had laid her body, then looking at mom. What did I feel? What was I supposed to feel? Loss? Despair? Regrets?

I felt nothing.

In truth, what emotions I did feel were for those around me who were struggling with the moment. Specifically I remember my niece having the hardest time. I tried to remember back to how I felt when Papa died. I had hoped to identify parallels that could help her cope. Both deaths were sudden, both were grandparents and we both shared those events as the first time losing someone close to you. I tried to console her, but my effort seemed to fall flat. My niece's parents and Shannon seemed to be connecting best with her so I just stood back and waited for everyone to say goodbye.

Following the viewing, a small group of us went to the local grocery store downtown to purchase all the food needed for our planned memorial service. Our plan was to secure a gazebo on a nearby lake and have an outdoor family meal where people could talk to each other about Janet and speak to the group. In a sense, we envisioned a supportive environment where family and friends could share their memories of mom. There wouldn't be a structure per se, more like a support group where anyone could give a eulogy. Janet loved the outdoors, she loved fellowship and she loved cookouts. Our mother was privately a very spiritual person. While it was known that she grew up Catholic and accepted Jesus as her savior, the mom I remember seemed most at peace when in tune with nature. With that in mind, we felt as a group that a memorial service put together outside spoke to who she was most strongly.

Starting with the previous day when much of the family had arrived and spilling over into the next day, there was a lot of discussion regarding when to hold the memorial service.

Dad was concerned that our plan to have it three days after her passing may have been a day or two early, he seemed most worried that on short notice some people would end up excluded. Collectively we reasoned with him that no matter what day you choose, someone won't be able to make it, he'd never make everybody happy. So, how about we do what worked best for the immediate family and do it while everybody who had already come would still be in town? Our logic seemed to make sense to dad, so the service was finalized for the following day, May 4th.

For the remainder of the day, May 3rd, most of our immediate family spent the day with dad. I would say the most difficult aspect for me in the early days of our family's loss was watching my dad figure out what his life would look like going forward. Simple tasks like figuring out how to manage meals or keep up with housework, promised to present challenges for him. Our mother, drunk or not, took care of dad. I'm not sure he made many of his own meals or washed his own clothes, the simple things. All of those little things a person might take for granted over the course of decades married could overwhelm him.

Privately I pulled my sister aside. When the week was over, everyone would return to their lives and move on. Only my sister with her family would remain. One character flaw I acknowledge was that sometimes my communication would come off condescending. I don't mean for it to, I think in part the issue arises from being detail oriented. No small detail is ever meaningless to me when dealing with adversity. Truly I valued my sister's role in our family, especially how she has cared for our dad. Her involvement and compassion for him I think has always been under appreciated. I have always been one of the worse in making sure her efforts were validated. With all of those thoughts in mind, when we sat down to chat I measured my words carefully.

"Sarah, when we leave, making sure dad is ok every day is going to fall in your lap. It's not fair, we all know you have a lot going on with two young kiddos, but it can't be helped. Please find a way to make sure he's not alone too much for a while and check on him frequently. Shannon and I will do what we can, which is little from so far away. I'm sorry, I wish we could do more."

Sarah, "I know Matt. Don't worry about it, we'll take care of him."

In my heart I knew, Sarah would do her best.

By late afternoon dad was exhausted with so many people smothering him. He politely asked everyone in his house to leave, he needed some space. My inner protector didn't want to leave, I wanted to stay so he wouldn't be alone. Then I thought about how I'd feel if so many people were in my face. Maybe the best thing for him would be some breathing room, some time to mourn his wife. Perhaps it would be best if we enabled him to have an evening to reflect before family surrounded him once again for the memorial service.

I hugged my dad and said, "We'll be a few miles away if you need someone. The time won't matter, call if you need me."

Dad promised he would.

While Shannon and I kept quiet for the rest of the night, I started thinking about what I wanted to say about mom for her memorial. Despite my emotional baggage, she deserved in death to at least have what was great about her memorialized. What could I say? I was not accustomed to viewing her in flattering ways. In truth, I had despised the woman alcohol had made her for so long, that as I tried to piece together some appropriate words all my eyes could see was red. Anger.

How could I force myself into a place I could not feel or believe to be true? Nobody would find my words authentic. Maybe it would be best if I would remain respectfully silent?

Fitfully I found sleep, maybe the morning would bring clarity.

***

Sunrise was still hours away when I woke up and found myself staring at the ceiling, deep in thought over what I wanted to say about my mother. I tried to recall moments from childhood that would paint her in a flattering picture. I remembered when I was little in Toppenish, she would set the coffee table upside down on the couch to vacuum and I would sit on top of the table, using the legs as flight controls. I remembered her bandaging my wounds after flipping my BMX in 3rd grade. I thought about the time she baked a shipment of cookies for me to share with fellow Marines for my birthday during our second Okinawa trip.

Yet, for every vague fond memory I could strain to recall, dozens upon dozens of memories played like photographs in my mind where the alcohol took priority. I recalled the terror of bouncing around the inside of a farm truck as it rolled through a field in the Yakima Valley. Silly crap like taking a hand-written note on my bicycle to a convenience store for cigarettes because she was too drunk to get them herself. Scores of instances where I would look to the stands after stealing bases in city ball and find my dad standing all alone. I remembered the frustration I felt after chucking dozens of beer cans into the bushes, only for them to be replaced the next day.

Unbidden, my thoughts trailed towards dad. I was not certain he would survive the loss. You hear about couples who stay together their whole lives, only to die close together, the survivors seem to perish from broken hearts.

I got mad all over again.

I had control over nothing, there was nothing I could do to help anyone or make anything better. Not even myself.

And finally, I began to sob.

As day four of life without mom began, tears poured and I couldn't stop them. I tried to stay quiet, but it was hopeless. Uncontrollable sobbing woke my wife. The harder I tried to choke back the tears and force composure, the louder I got. Shannon just rolled over and hugged me, she didn't say a word. I just laid there with my back to her and cried through convulsions.

When the kaleidoscope of emotions had run through their natural course I was finally able to focus. As if a fog had lifted, I knew what needed to be said.

Shannon asked if I was ok.

I said, "Yeah I'm ok. I want to give the first eulogy."

***

While the rest of the world was still waking up, I found my brother at his hotel room across the way from where Shannon and I were. "Good morning John. Would you be ok with me giving the first eulogy?"

John and Sarah always seemed closer to mom than I had been, simply controlling the entire day was the last thing I wanted. Sharing their grief and respecting their desires was very important throughout the process. If my siblings had arranged some tribute I was not aware of, it would have been inconsiderate and rude to invalidate them.

My brother looked at me thoughtfully and said, "Yeah Matt, that will be alright."

A few hours later Shannon, John and his family, and myself were the first to arrive at the memorial sight. Hours ahead of time, still we wanted to make sure the gazebo was secured since it was first come. Shortly thereafter, my sister Sarah arrived with her family. As with my brother I asked for her consent to speak first. She graciously approved.

Within a few hours, most of the people who were expected to attend mom's memorial had arrived. As we had thought, the day was going exactly how mom might have liked. There were tears and fellowship as each person greeted the other. Far more apparent to me at least was a feeling of empathy and gratitude for one another. Dad had brought a number of pictures which he situated on one table in tribute.

Then there was food, so much food. Children were running around between the gazebo and beach. Mom would have loved that as well.

Finally, after everyone had arrived and greeted each other, I called for attention from all who had come. I thanked everyone for coming on behalf of our father and my siblings. With a deep breath, I spoke from the heart:

"One of the character traits I loved most about my mom was her connection with nature. If you knew her, then you know that not only did she adore all animals, she loved everything mother Earth provided. Since my earliest days, mom had always enjoyed gardening, tomatoes anything that needed water and soil. If it could grow, she wanted to nurture it. Regardless of what way you find God, we are all spiritual in nature. I personally happen to believe that God exists within us and all around us. When I see the trees, the grass or flowers I see God. When I see our children running up and down this beach, I see the hand of God in their joy. I believe mom was the same way, I believe she found peace and harmony in the abundance surrounding us. Since I happen to believe that heaven is here on Earth, and that all you have to do is look, then in every direction I look right now her presence is evident."

Amazingly I did not cry during my little monologue. In fact, while I was paying our mother tribute, I had a secondary purpose for the way I chose to eulogize her. Dad was listening. I wanted him to see hope. I wanted him to see his love for the woman he loved every time he opened his eyes. I'm not sure I could have ever forgiven my mom if the man I had idolized since boyhood died prematurely over her.

Chapter 24

Months later, back in Oklahoma, the first anthology from Books by Vets was nearing completion. 'Walk with Warriors' was nearly fully realized. Numerous submissions were made from all over the country, to read these stories veterans were submitting was a real honor. Had we as an infant organization saved anybody yet? Who knows. What I do know is that for the select handful of men and women who submitted work, their transparency, vulnerability and belief in our vision meant a great deal to Shannon and me.

Late in the editing process one veteran changed his mind and backed out while another had ended up writing a piece that read as anti-American. Shannon and I discussed the chapter in question and came to the conclusion that including a chapter like that, no matter how well written, would be a disservice to all the other authors and was not consistent with the tone of the project. Instead, Shannon offered to help him individually in sharing his story.

Our decision to omit a chapter left us with one small issue. Built into the structure of the project was the unique quality that 22 authors each contributed a chapter, a number chosen intentionally to raise awareness for the 22 service men and women who take their lives each day. Leaving out the final submission left the book with 21 chapters, and the book was up against a deadline.

Shannon was concerned about finding another veteran to get a near publish worthy chapter submitted on short notice. We put our heads together in an attempt to manifest a veteran out of thin air who would want to get involved.

Unfortunately, Books by Vets was still an infant in the world of charitable organizations. We weren't well known and the only exposure there had been up until then had been through social media.

I knew Shannon needed my help. To find a relatively polished piece within a few days from someone who wanted to get involved wasn't impossible, just incredibly difficult. As luck would have it, I had actually already started writing as part of an unrelated project. For many years I had toyed with the idea of writing a book about my time in the Marines. I had already written an introduction for it. So, observing Shannon's stress level I offered, "Sweetheart, I could write you a chapter. I don't suffer from PTSD, so I'm not necessarily representative of what we're looking for, but I could write about my reasoning for joining the Corps and some of the adversity I dealt with early on."

Looking at the face of my wife was very satisfying. Now, I'm not trying to make a bigger deal about this than it was, but in a small way I was saving her. Credibility early on was very important to gain traction and give legitimacy to our message. I asked her to give me until the following evening.

The next morning I sat down and wrote the final chapter to 'Walk with Warriors.' In the chapter I talked about the roles dad and Papa played in my decision to join the Marines. I covered ROTC rejecting me, Papa's death and Taps before finally figuring out my motivation for surviving when self-doubt closed in. Fortunately, my work ended up requiring only a few edits and Shannon was able to finish our first book for Books by Vets.

'Walk with Warriors' released in July of 2017. A launch party was held in downtown OKC and Shannon was even able to get a TV interview on one of the local channels to promote the book.

Among our concerns shortly after releasing the book was how best to raise money to continue our mission. While book sales were encouraging, it was apparent that we'd need to raise more money than book sales alone provided. We needed to establish Books by Vets as a non-profit so that meaningful funds could be collected to help vets on the levels we foresaw.

Toward the end of 2017 Shannon had assembled a board for Books by Vets. One of the board members and his wife donated the funds to officially legitimize Books by Vets' non-profit status. With the help of the board, Books by Vets established goals and future projects. 'Resilient Warriors' was set for 2018, a second anthology, this time comprised entirely of female veterans. The time had arisen for raising public awareness to fund 'Resilient' and other books to follow.

***

Shannon and the board decided to hold a launch party in the spring of 2018, officially announcing Books by Vets to the community and world as a non-profit whose sole mission it was to reduce the number 22 to 0.

Turnout for the event was exceptionally good. We sold out of copies of 'Walk with Warriors' in the first half hour or so. Those who attended were very generous with their donations as well. Shannon and the entire board had a chance to introduce themselves before the microphone was turned over to contributing authors in 'Walk with Warriors' to talk about what writing had done for them.

I had not anticipated speaking that night. In truth I had planned only on doing whatever needed doing to remove stress from my wife. Shannon had worked very long hours for many months with no compensation to get Books by Vets realized. All I wanted for the evening was for Shannon to focus on organizational growth. So, you might imagine, that when I was asked to address the crowd about my chapter I was taken by surprise.

My speech was completely off the cuff, not even scripted a little. I brought attention to the veterans out there who say, "I don't know what to say. I never saw combat; my story doesn't matter." I believe the purpose of my involvement was to give a voice to those who don't initially see value in their service. I never saw combat. I missed Somalia by a year on the front end of my enlistment and Afghanistan by three months on the back end. I routinely suffer with survivor guilt. When I find myself in dark places, one of the regrets I punish myself with is failing to rejoin the Corps following the 9/11 attacks. So I spoke primarily about identifying adversity in your life and how we learn to adapt and overcome it.

Unbeknownst to me, following my speech, a critical new relationship was fermenting. A man by the name of Mac Mullings introduced himself to my wife. He told Shannon about the radio show he co-hosted in OKC and asked my wife if she'd like to come on for an interview to talk about what Books by Vets does. After accepting the interview,

Mac asked her to bring me along, apparently he'd found me entertaining and interesting.

***

Two weeks after the non-profit launched publicly, Shannon and I appeared on 'The Ride' with Mac Mullings and his co-host to talk Books by Vets. Up until that day, my role with Books by Vets had really been more behind the scenes so to speak. While the actual founding was partially my credit, Shannon did all the work. I didn't even meddle with board business, really you could say I was simply a volunteer. So when Shannon insisted I come along for the radio interview I was uncomfortable.

"Shannon, why do I need to be there? Isn't this about Books by Vets? Why don't you bring a member of the board?'"

Shannon, "Sweetheart, Mac asked for you by name. He liked what you had to say at the launch. Besides, I want you there with me."

True to my introverted nature, I grumbled and complained before finally acquiescing.

We ended up staying on for two segments. Shannon and Mac bantered back and forth for a majority of our time on the air; discussing our founding, mission, books and the veterans themselves. Shannon and I learned a little about what made Mac Mullings a fan of ours as well. His father was a veteran who had been integral in getting veteran memorials built until he had only recently passed away. I remember Mac saying, "If only my pops had a chance like this before he passed...I wonder what it could have done for him and the family?"

Mac turned to me a number of times to keep me involved in the interview. We talked a little about my speech a few weeks prior and my message. He asked me about my parents. I talked about my dad and his chapter in 'Walk with Warriors' before delving into my chapter.

At the end of the second segment, during the commercial break, we shook hands, took a picture and then Mac invited us to come on for his weekend show, 'Rise Above with Mac Mullings.' Rise Above is a show Mac hosts on Saturdays for two hours in which he talks about addiction and recovery. Mac is himself, in recovery and not without tests. He was given his one-year coin just a single day before the loss of his father. What role could Books by Vets play in the recovery community? Many vets turn to substance abuse in order to cope with depression, PTSD and other issues. Maybe Books by Vets could reach some of those vets. We agreed to commit to a two-hour Rise Above. Again, Mac requested I attend.

Several weeks after our first radio interview, Shannon and I appeared on 'Rise Above' with Mac Mullings to discuss; Books by Vets, addiction and recovery, 'Walk with Warriors', future projects like 'Resilient' and much more. This time I was more comfortable and engaged in the discussion. During a commercial break I asked Mac if it would be alright to talk about my mom and her alcoholism regarding the role she played in my decisions. Mac said, "Yeah man let's do it."

Returning from break, Mac asked the question about why I joined the Marines. Considering Rise Above is about addiction and finding recovery, I was finally able to organically tell my story. "Mac, I grew up with one of my parents being an addict, alcoholism. My mom was a terrible alcoholic. I had lofty goals and expectations for myself, joining the Marines wasn't my plan. I wanted to go to college. I dreamed of being a fighter pilot. Due in part to my mom's addiction, I couldn't get financial help for things as simple as college applications. I wasn't asking for tuition, we're talking scholarship applications. ROTC rejected me when I applied despite good grades. Staying around the house with a drunk while I re-applied had no appeal to me. I just wanted out, so I joined the Marines to escape."

I think what set me apart from other guests Mac was accustomed to having on was my perspective. Typically, a majority of the people who appear on Rise Above Radio are in recovery. I was unique because for lack of a better word I was a *victim* of addiction. My desired course of life was altered by a parent whose addiction was out of control. Anger and resentment had consumed me to the point where my vision for other alternatives saw no path besides simply escaping. I didn't understand addiction, and frankly I didn't want to. Deep down I felt that forgiving or validating my mom for how I'd grown up would somehow legitimize her choices. I wanted to forgive my mom, I knew that holding on to anger wasn't healthy. Where I struggled most was, I knew it was wrong to cling to the past, but how could I forgive a person who had shown no remorse for how her addiction had impacted me? Therein was the central point of my conflict. Balance. My mother never once made apologies for her addiction and how it affected me known, so without remorse there could not be forgiveness.

So as we sat there in that interview with Mac Mullings, I wanted to hog him to myself. I wanted someone who understood addiction to hear me and understand me. I wanted to be validated. I wanted my mom to say, "I'm sorry that you missed out on your dreams." I didn't want to hate. I didn't want to be resentful. I WANTED to forgive. I simply had no clue how I could achieve reconciliation with a parent who never showed remorse and was dead.

I feared I would be stuck in emotional purgatory forever.

***

Following our appearance on Mac's show, I made a regular habit of tuning into Rise Above. While I am not an addict myself, listening became therapeutic for me in a strange way. Almost as if hearing strangers who have chosen recovery over self destruction would give me insight into a life that could have been. A quasi alternate universe if you could imagine it. Many guests on Rise Above had hit rock bottom and recovery was giving them a second chance at life.

I found it refreshing and uplifting.

Additionally, there was Mac Mullings himself. I like Mac for a few reasons. First, he had supported the vision Shannon and I had with Books by Vets. Perhaps more importantly though, I found him authentic. Mac doesn't carry himself like a big shot radio guy. Rather, the guy you hear is the man he is; humble, transparent and willing to be vulnerable.

So, I challenged myself to listen with an open mind in hopes of gaining understanding of my mom. Not that I expected Mac and his guests to speak for my mom strictly speaking, it's just that many of the people I heard, including Mac, drank like mom did. I heard all the familiar themes; hiding addiction, priority of drinking over family, refusing to see the problem with addiction, and having little regard for those who were affected around them. With each passing guest I heard a lot of these same behaviors.

One theme I was not familiar with surfaced, however. Something I had not heard or considered specifically in relation to my mom. Many of the people I listened to who had chosen recovery had initially turned to alcohol or drugs to medicate some kind of trauma. Types of trauma could differ from case to case. Some examples included: death of a loved one, divorce, significant losses and sexual abuse. I began to wonder; *was my mom dealing with some kind of trauma I was not aware of?*

June 2, 2018 Mac Mullings and Rise Above Radio hosted a man by the name of Brian Anderson. Brian is clinical director for a recovery center in the Oklahoma City area. Brian Anderson is also in recovery. Brian has a family and is a veteran. Brian was very candid, listening to his story of recovery and how his life has turned around to the point he helps others now was riveting to hear about. What was most remarkable and memorable about Brian for me was a short exchange he had with Mac as the show was wrapping up.

Mac, "So what are your regrets? What do you struggle with?"

Brian, "I regret most the impact my addiction had on my family. I wish I hadn't put my family through that."

Now, Brian Anderson and my mom have little enough in common. Clearly their stories are very different. However, in that moment, it was as if mom was speaking to me through Brian from the beyond.

Here's what I heard, *"Matt, I'm stubborn and proud. Though I've never said so to you, I'm sorry for putting you through alcoholism. I'm sorry for hurting you."*

I pulled my vehicle over right then and there. And then, I cried. Loud and hard, I cried. I ugly cried. I cried until my eyes ran dry and I had to focus on breathing. On June 2, 2018, almost thirteen months to the day after she had died, I finally missed my mom.

For the first time in my life, I wanted to call my mom.

June 2, 2018 I finally began to grieve my loss.

Chapter 25

How do you heal a broken relationship when half of those involved have died?

Books by Vets was founded to help veterans find peace and heal through writing. While that mission statement focuses primarily on those who are battling PTSD, I wondered if maybe the best avenue to find my answers could be found through writing some things down. Maybe I could be the person Shannon and I had initially set out to find.

For starters, I wrote down a page of questions specific to my upbringing that I would seek answers to. Next, I would call everyone I could who was close to my mom at some point in an effort to piece together who the real Janet Whittington was. Central focus of my effort would be to identify the 'why.' In my heart, I could not believe someone would really drink themselves to death over the course of nearly 50 years just because it was fun. The 'why' was there, in plain sight if only I asked the right questions to the right people.

I began my search for understanding with my dad. My initial batch of questions proved to be ineffective, or at least not specific enough for me to get the answers I was looking for from my dad. The most useful insight I gleaned from dad was, "Your mom just wanted people to accept her for who she was because that's what she did for others."

My dad's answer to 'why' was, "Because she enjoyed it and your mom is her father's daughter."

While that logic worked for my father, I rejected it out of hand. In my mind, cop out. I'm my mother's son, so...can you see where this line of thinking falls apart?

At the risk of being rude, I thought, *mom deserves a better understanding than blaming genetics.* If I had learned anything from listening to dozens of people in various stages of recovery, there is almost always a reason or trauma. I'll not just simply accept that her addiction lacked a trigger moment. Some source of pain that she used alcohol as a means to numb. While I believe some who knew her saw sense in Janet saying she "enjoyed it", what I believe she truly enjoyed was how it made her feel. How the booze drowned out whatever was bothering her. Whatever turmoil she dealt with in life, beer was the answer. Mom learned at some point through some trauma the magical effect alcohol had on dealing with tough emotional issues.

I turned to some of mom's siblings.

I messaged one of my mother's sisters and asked for a good time to talk on the phone. Within a day or so I was on the phone with her. I started out by assuring my aunt about my intentions. Truly I had no desire to dig up reasons to find faults in my mom. I assured her I was looking for redemption. I told my aunt, "What I'm trying to do is get myself to a place of forgiveness. I don't want to be angry anymore, all the anger I've carried for so long serves no purpose. I want to know if my mom regretted the harm she did her kids. I also am looking for the why. Why would she not quit? Why would she drink herself to death?"

Aunt, "Well Matthew, you know your mom was sexually assaulted when we were younger don't you?"

My heart stopped. Wait, what did she just say?

Me, "What?! No!"

Aunt, "Yes, Matthew, one of our older brothers sexually assaulted your mom. I thought you knew?"

Me, "No I didn't know! So, you mean like .... raped?!"

Aunt, "I don't know the exact details, but it was pretty bad."

Me, "Wait, so .... tell me more"

Aunt, "Matthew I know you think very fondly of your Nana and Papa so I don't want to...."

Me, "Please, I need to hear it."

Aunt, "Well, your mom was afraid to tell Papa out of fear for what he might do to our brother. So, your mom went and told Nana what had happened. Basically, your mom was told, it's done and over. Nothing can be done by telling anyone else. More or less she was told that the law need not get involved and she should just move on."

Me, "So, the brother didn't get in trouble?!"

Aunt, "Times were different then. Things like this weren't discussed. Issues were handled within the family."

42 years later, I finally had the why.

Simple as a finger snap, my anger vanished. My resentment vanished. Years of confusion and frustration over being in the middle of an emotional fog and suddenly there was clarity. Mom absolutely had a trigger event. She absolutely had a reason to drown herself in booze. A betrayal so diabolical, so perverted and so senseless from which there is no path to validation. How could she find peace and validation when her own family failed her? Her own mother! Her own mother assigned priority to a perverted son rather than sticking up for a vulnerable daughter looking for justice.

Her mother, my Nana failed her.

Her, own, mother!

I was beyond incensed. Angry all over again. This time not at my mom, but at myself. How could I be so selfish, so narrow minded, so stuck in my own world to not be open to asking my own mom while she lived, 'Mom, why?"

What if she would have told me? How could our relationship have been different? How could I have developed and grown differently? What about my own sexual abuse as a teen? We had that in common!!! We could have found understanding in each other! What a waste!

Mom and I shared similar traumas from our teen years. Thinking back to those interviews with law enforcement, she had to know what was going on. Why stay quiet? Why leave me alone in my thoughts? She knew what I was going through, why did she choose to back off instead of stepping up?

I was beyond angry. I was fed up with this old-world mafia bullshit where nobody ever talked about anything. *Your*

mom is her father's daughter. If you mean suppression of trauma over the course of a lifetime through alcohol abuse and stubborn ass refusal to get help, then
yes, I finally see what you mean.

I called another of my mom's siblings, this time I knew exactly the questions to ask. For the sake of validating my mom in her death, I felt it would be important to hear the story of her abuse from more than one person.

Cross-checking facts if you will.

I asked another of my mom's sisters if she knew anything about the abuse Janet had suffered and how she was affected. Once again, I heard the whole story. Completely the same story. This time I was given a little more insight. "Matthew, I know your mom struggled with that sexual assault and the fact that our parents didn't do anything about it. Anytime the family would get together for Christmas years later, when our brother would show up, it re-traumatized her all over again. When our brother died, she was relieved."

Wow. I got angry all over yet again! Not only was she never heard, mom had to subject herself to him at family functions over and over and over again. How could she ever heal those wounds? At what point was she ever in control? To be forced into familial obligations over and over with the very people who violated your innocence and told you through actions, *you're not important enough to stick up for.*

No wonder she drank so much.

I wanted to fight for her.

Who else knew about this?

I called my dad, he knew. I called my sister and brother, they both knew.

How in the hell did I not know?

The answer hit me like a freight train. *Matt, you weren't told because you isolated yourself. Rather than showing compassion and empathy, you showed intolerance and judgement. What would you expect? The Golden Rule. You broke it.*

Not that I presume in having the power of absolution, but in the course of only a few days through asking the right people the right questions, all that I had held onto in the way of anger for so long was gone. When I thought about my mom, I cried, a lot. In my car, alone, is where I grieved most often.

All that I had found wrong in my mom before was seen anew through the lens of understanding. While I personally have found other ways to cope with difficulties in my life, including a sexual assault, it doesn't make me better than her. Just different. I wished she would have been
humble enough to get help rather than use alcohol. Maybe she had the opportunity, maybe she didn't. Perhaps since nobody gave her the understanding she craved, she may have assumed counseling would have been pointless. Maybe she tried to talk about the real issues while under the influence and every person who she came in contact with simply dismissed her as a babbling drunk.

All speculation of course.

What is certain?

I had finally found the path to understanding my mom and letting go of anger. She was simply drinking to survive her demons. What is there to resent when I ended up doing pretty good in life? So I didn't get to be a fighter pilot or go to college, so what? What had I achieved? What good things had I done? Who had I uplifted along the way? Instead of looking for mistakes and shortcomings, I started to see positivity around me. Rather than being quick to anger and judgement I find myself finding common ground and understanding.

Rather than seeing addiction and hopelessness in a person, I see pain and feel the desire to strive for acceptance.

Above all else, along this long and painful journey I found myself finally saying quietly to all things nature around me, "I forgive you mom."

Chapter 26

Often I have described to people how I viewed my mom in the past as, "Seeing her actions and behaviors through this 'red veil of anger'". So, when Brian Anderson said that one of his primary regrets was the harm done to his family, it was as if I was finally given permission to believe my mom felt bad for being addicted to alcohol. What my mind really needed in order to allow myself to forgive was the belief in the possibility she felt remorse.

Once I understood her potential 'why', forgiveness came for me. I wanted to believe mom didn't like drinking, didn't like the harm she did to herself and didn't like the harm she did to her kids. This is important because the decision to share her trauma in this book was a difficult one for me. In part, I felt that she kept it private for a reason and who am I to make the decision for her to go public? Ultimately, I felt it was necessary to share her story as part of mine for a few reasons. First thought that came to my mind was my own sexual trauma. The fact that she stayed silent in the moment of time where I was dealing with sexual abuse is a real tragedy. I hope other people out there who are struggling with addiction due to sexual trauma can learn from this. Turn your pain into something positive, especially if someone close is made to deal with a similar tragedy. I believe my mom missed an excellent opportunity back in my teenage years to build better understanding with me.

Secondly, to understand her pain could be the key to understanding her addiction. I cannot presume to say that her abuse was the sole cause of her alcoholism, but to say it was not a factor would be arrogant and naïve for those looking to dismiss her. I wanted to put it in the book, not to embarrass or dishonor anyone; rather it was paramount to validate my mother. The day of reckoning for those who worked to suppress her voice has arrived. I cannot in good conscience endorse further behavior that buries painful truths. My mother deserved justice, in some small measure, I hope I have given her that in death. Her story has finally been heard and perhaps now she can be understood a little better.

In truth, I have put a great deal of thought into how this story would be digested by those closest to mom. Anytime prior to Brian Anderson's appearance on Rise Above, when someone would ask or talk about my mom, that 'red veil' would come over me and my emotions went to a place of anger. A place where, once there, I could not see redeeming qualities in my mother. I was simply blind to them. If someone tried to contradict my perception of anger, I could not be reasonable, the resentment was too strong. So, it was important to me that while going through the process of interviewing people, I made concerted efforts to draw out all the positivity I could gather about mom in the memories of those who loved her.

Universally my mom is remembered for being exceptionally tolerant in the flaws of those she knew. Janet was known to forgive quickly in most circumstances, the only exception that seemed to plague her was hypocrisy. I found that trait very interesting since hypocrisy and self-righteousness tend to spike my ire as well. Mom was also very personable, outside of the home especially. I could not find a single person who disliked working with her. In fact, I found through my dad that not only was my mom well liked at work, she was very accomplished when tasked with responsibility and asked to tackle challenges. Specifically, while working for the Navy exchange, she received many awards from the Navy.

I found that in her conversations with other loved ones, she frequently expressed authentic compassion and interest for what was going on in the lives of others. Oftentimes she would listen with great interest without trying to force her own issues and family stories. In those recollections, I saw a woman who could exhibit great amounts of selflessness and in the cases where she saw adversity, empathy. Two traits that I have sorely lacked for much of my life.

Mom was very proud of the family she had made with my dad. Despite my vitriolic departure from home for the Marines, all who I spoke to say she only beamed with pride and loved giving updates to anyone who would listen about what I had going on in the Corps. A revelation that frankly stunned me. I expected that mom would find ways to minimize or ignore completely what I was doing while gone in the Marines. The exact opposite was true. In that respect, my mom was a far better person than me. She seemed to not hold a grudge against me for leaving, mom found pride in my service.

Maybe one of the hardest challenges I have had since leaving home has been seeing shortcomings in my father. In her death, my dad has disclosed some of his struggles. My dad has some regrets of his own in terms of what kind of husband he was. To mom's credit, she was quick to forgive my father's errors and only asked for acceptance in return. Like myself, dad was slow to forgive her addiction.

With each passing interview, I noticed a trend or consistency. Every single person regretted failing to make more of an effort in reserving judgement and seeing the real Janet. Every single person I spoke with was clinging to some small measure of guilt. Every single time I gave people the chance to recall what they loved about Janet, they cried and gushed about how loving a woman she was. Every single person told me they had found difficulty in grieving her loss and because of our conversations, felt better.

***

While in the midst of figuring out who my mom really was and why addiction plagued her right up to her demise, an emotion overcame me like it had so many others, guilt.

Guilt over how I treated my mom and failing to be the compassionate person I fancied myself to be really consumed me. Nobody has been harder on me than, well me. Guilt over the fact that I made this mom out to be a selfish drunken demon, who only ever cared about herself, kids and family be damned. Man, was I ever a hypocrite and an asshole.

My own mother didn't trust enough to confide in me one of the darkest episodes of her life yet shared it with everyone else. Why? Because I judged her and told her she was worthless through my own actions, that's why. Would you entrust in someone your vulnerabilities and darkest fears if that person has done nothing but tear you down? Tell you how much of a lousy drunk you are? Tell you that YOU are the reason he'd rather die for his country than spend one more day in your presence?

Would you want a person like that in your life?

I wouldn't.

So, what do you do when the person you dislike the most is yourself?

I had no idea how to process my guilt. Naturally I feel the need to tell my mom how sorry I am. Apologies are far more difficult to make when the person you feel the need to square things up with has passed on. For me, the apology just sticks in my throat, she can't hear me. Mom was gone long before I figured out in time the path of forgiveness. She never heard me say the words to her. I can never make that right.

This very imbalance had kept me in a perpetual state of self hate for months, until I finally admitted the issues were above my ability to find solutions for. Finally, with a little help from Shannon, I admitted to myself that I in fact, needed outside help.

I started going to counseling while still in the early stages of writing this book. I had previously used counseling while still in Minnesota to heal after Britney had left. It was there I learned a lot about myself. I learned what it meant to be introverted. I learned a lot about grief and how I cope with losses. I learned that rather than pointing fingers, I tended to assign a lot of blame on myself (except in things concerning my mom, back then.) So, I had confidence that with the right professional, solutions could be found and I could achieve equilibrium again.

I found a grief counselor who really seemed to understand my struggles, a counselor who truly understood addiction and the resulting effects on children, her name is Madison Mills. For the first few weeks, all we discussed was my mom and past relationships. Before long, Madison was able to see how much I beat myself up for things I had done, how I treated people and mistakes I made. She said, "Matt you need to forgive. What you've lived through is traumatic, expecting that you can simply flip a switch and have everything be good again isn't realistic."

I said, "But I HAVE forgiven my mom. I'm truly not angry anymore, I wish she hadn't been an alcoholic but I don't have anger over that anymore. Now I'm really angry at myself. I'm really disappointed in myself."

Madison said, "I don't mean forgive your mom, you need to forgive yourself."

How do you forgive yourself?

I told her, "I don't know how. I feel like the biggest hypocrite. I feel like I've been all the awful things to my mom that I accused her of being to me. I feel selfish. I feel like I'm just a big selfish know it all asshole. Besides I feel like I need my mom's forgiveness, and how do I get that when she's dead? How can I ever balance this out?"

Forgive yourself she said.

How does one achieve self-forgiveness? That would be a neat little trick. So, I just say, "Sorry Matt and grant forgiveness to myself?" I knew she was right and it sounds healthy, but it is much harder than it sounds.

More difficult even than forgiving my mom.

***

I'm still not sure exactly when I'll know that I have forgiven myself. In part I believe that life is a journey in forgiveness. Nobody is perfect, nobody. Even a person who may be considered universally evil doesn't wake up and say, "I'm going to see if I can make even more people hate me today. Oh, and maybe I'll kill a few puppies."

No, people inherently strive to be the best versions of themselves that they feel capable of being. Someone who is addicted to alcohol may only be trying to survive the battle raging in their own minds. An alcoholic doesn't start a day off trying to destroy everyone they love; an alcoholic is self-medicating.

I forgave my second wife for her addiction to alcohol faster than I forgave my mom for a lifetime of it, yet I found forgiveness. I found forgiveness for my mom because the right people came into my life who were able to help me lift a veil of anger so that I could see what I was too stubborn to look for. Why? The right people taught me that addiction truly is a disease and it takes different forms. In fact, I was taught that addiction is the only disease that tries to convince you that nothing is wrong. Mom probably never saw herself as having something wrong because the booze her body needed made all her pain go away.

Amazingly, once I learned to forgive my mom, other issues I had with other people became meaningless and easy to forgive. I'm happier now that I have learned how good it feels to let go and forgive people.

In reflection, after months of working on this book and countless times I've broken down in tears I've learned that forgiving is not forgetting. Forgiveness simply heals wounds that one has chosen to keep bare and replaces broken memories with renewed hope for future growth. You don't forget, rather, simply see things in a fresh way.

Will I ever forgive myself for how I treated my mother? I sincerely hope so. I don't intend to beat myself up for the rest of my life. Instead, I would like to think that reflecting on how I evolved to this point could help someone else. My ultimate hope, is that someone out there who has grown up in similar circumstances, will read this and find a way to achieve peace in their life.

"To forgive is the highest, most beautiful form of love. In return, you will receive untold peace and happiness." -
Robert Muller

Acknowledgments

There are many reasons for the timing of my story. When you boil it all down though, a primary factor emerges; the right people had to intersect into my life. I would like to take a moment to acknowledge them now for their help in this evolution.

For starters I would like to say thank you to my test readers; Blythe Donovan, Asa Leveaux, Travis Johnson and Patty Quick. Funny thing about writing a story about yourself, you already know it. Paramount of importance to me was finding a small group of people who were not in my mind or in direct contact with a majority of the events in order to identify the holes I left and assumptions in knowledge that I presumed while writing. Feedback from these selfless people was key to bringing you this story.

Dillon Cooper of the non-profit, No Surrender, photographed the cover. Dillon's presence on this Earth and within the network of people who I have chosen to surround myself with is truly a blessing. A selfless man who seems to truly enjoy uplifting all those he comes in contact with. Thank you for the awesome work on my cover Dillon.

At one point while writing I became hopelessly stuck. In part, because by the time I had actually started writing meaningful chapters, I had already found forgiveness for my mom. Yet, I was incredibly imbalanced, emotional and confused. Almost as if I had lost part of my identity. Additionally, around that time, a terrible tragedy befell a boy in my local area due to an alcoholic parent's negligence. I elected to seek out counseling to work through some stuff and as I wrote about earlier, I found out how stuck I was within myself. Pools of guilt and anger towards myself were deep and complicated. Madison Mills, a wonderful grief counselor, helped me more than she knows. Through Madison I have learned, and continue to work on daily, that accepting my errors and forgiving them, while difficult is incredibly necessary.

If not for Brian Anderson, who changed my life with one simple sentence, it may have taken me many more months or years to get where I am today. Sure, I projected how my mother may have felt in his place yet wrapping my mind around the possibility of her remorse allowed me to be vulnerable and finally forgive.

Many people in my life have tried to encourage acceptance and forgiveness. People I have loved. People I have respected. People I trust. Even Shannon tried to give me nudges along the way, getting here took a very special catalyst. Mac Mullings changed my life, forever and for the better. Among the many attributes I love and admire most about my friend Mac are his transparency, vulnerability and above all his humility. Mac makes no excuses for his past, especially regarding his struggles with addiction. Like me, he arrived at a very low point. What he did next altered the course of his life and all those he touches. In his own words, he submitted himself to a higher power, God. Mac admitted that he couldn't solve his struggle with addiction alone and he got help. By his own admissions he was fearful that his daughter may have to grow up without him, so changes were made. Now, Mac touches countless people who have chosen recovery through his show, Rise Above. Specifically, when he and I discussed my mom, I was worried that he wouldn't see value in this story through the eyes of the person affected by addiction. I feared that he would make excuses and try to force feed tolerance down my throat like many people in my life had. I was very wrong. Instead I received validation. I received understanding. I received the gift of empowerment. When I told Mac I didn't want to be angry, and that I knew my emotions were illogical and wrong he did not correct me. He loved me. By his actions I could feel kinship. Authentic kinship. So I did what I had been unable to do for a lifetime, I listened. Mac Mullings has not only fostered the environment that taught me forgiveness, since I have finally let decades of anger go, my cups are overflowing with acceptance and happiness. In cases where in the past I may have chosen anger and judgement, now I most often find myself striving to uplift others.

Finally I would like to say how grateful I am to have Shannon Whittington as my wife and best friend. While Shannon was not the one who ultimately revealed my path to forgiveness, she certainly hacked away a lot of the bushes obscuring it. Early on in our relationship I was very candid about the dynamic between me and mom. So much so that I felt my honesty risked scaring her off. Still, I felt that while developing a bond with a partner, honesty over an issue this significant is important. To truly understand me, one would have to be able to understand how I felt about my mom. Effects from my relationship with mom spread through all aspects of my life, like deep roots through a garden. Shannon may not have necessarily appreciated the whole picture early on, but what she did better than anyone could have, was remain open to understanding without judgement. Even her attempts at encouraging a more positive relationship with mom were gentle and good natured. Really what mattered most to Shannon was my happiness. She knew I would never truly be happy until I figured mom out. Sadly mom died before actually meeting Shannon face to face. My wife does countless things that contribute to my emotional health. Of the utmost importance of all the little things she does is, Shannon embraces with full acceptance and love the real Matt. She doesn't try to change me or make me into the version of Matt people think I ought to be. Sounds so simple doesn't it? I'm not clay to be molded, I'm a real man with real character quirks that make me unique. My lovely wife just loves me as is, and that is what makes her more special to me than anyone I've ever met. Lest I forget to mention, this book would have literally been impossible without her. Writing and sharing stories is quite literally her passion. All the little things a novice writer doesn't think about when trying to get a book to print, Shannon either walked me through or did it for me. You have read this book because of Shannon Whittington.

For more information about effects alcoholism can have on children, specifically regarding development and inheritance of addiction please get on a computer and check out this hyperlink:

https://americanaddictioncenters.org/alcoholism-treatment/children/

If you are struggling with addiction yourself, especially if you are raising children, please know that someone out there wants to help you. Someone wants to hear you out and validate your pain. You don't have to remain trapped in addiction, recovery is possible. YOU have to WANT it.

Thank you for reading Forgiven.

CPSIA information can be obtained
at www.ICGtesting.com
Printed in the USA
FFHW011409020219
50407069-55569FF